Managing Multiple Projects

Other titles in the Briefcase Books series include:

To learn more about titles in the Briefcase Books series go to
www.briefcasebooks.com

You'll find the tables of contents, downloadable sample chapters, information on the authors, discussion guides for using these books in training programs, and more.

A Briefcase Book

Managing Multiple Projects

Michael Tobis
Irene P. Tobis

McGraw-Hill
New York Chicago San Francisco Lisbon London
Madrid Mexico City Milan New Delhi San Juan
Seoul Singapore Sydney Toronto

McGraw-Hill

A Division of The McGraw·Hill Companies

4 5 6 7 8 9 0 AGM/AGM 0 9 8 7 6 5 4 3

ISBN 0-07-138896-6

Library of Congress Cataloging-in-Publication Data applied for.

This is a CWL Publishing Enterprises Book, developed and produced for McGraw-Hill by CWL Publishing Enterprises, John A. Woods, President. For more information, contact CWL Publishing Enterprises, 3010 Irvington Way, Madison, WI 53713-3414, www.cwlpub.com. Robert Magnan served as editor. For McGraw-Hill, the sponsoring editor is Catherine Dassopoulos, and the publisher is Jeffrey Krames.

Printed and bound by Quebecor World Martinsburg.

This publication is designed to provide accurate and authoritative information in regard to the subject matter covered. It is sold with the understanding that neither the author nor the publisher is engaged in rendering legal, accounting, or other professional service. If legal advice or other expert assistance is required, the services of a competent professional person should be sought.
> *—From a Declaration of Principles jointly adopted by a Committee of the American Bar Association and a Committee of Publishers*

Contents

Preface

Many managers find themselves trying to figure out how to meet the demands of the multiple projects, roles, and responsibilities that compete for their attention. It's not something most have been trained to do. Thus this book.

We've designed it to help you to meet the challenges, both technical and psychological, of being responsible for many things that are being done by several people. This is especially the case in today's knowledge-driven workplace, where many of us face a wide divergence of types and sizes of projects.

While books and tools abound for managing large group projects and also for improving personal productivity, the marketplace currently offers surprisingly little help for the manager of a small workgroup faced with a wide range of responsibilities. Often today's manager is juggler—responsible for keeping numerous balls in the air and never disappointing the audience. Those balls are often small and medium-sized projects that need to be completed on time and on spec so the manager can then get on with the next projects. All this is combined with the need to fulfill other ongoing responsibilities. How you do this effectively is not addressed in business school. But now there is help because that is precisely the topic of this book.

Managing Multiple Projects will help you improve individual and group skills as you cope with competing demands for your attention and effort.

The approaches offered here are based on our extensive experience helping managers and small workgroups in a variety of settings. Our strategies have helped our clients to overcome overload and frustration and to move on to enjoyable and sustainable productivity. These strategies, which draw upon our backgrounds in systems engineering and psychology, can help you, too.

This is not a "one size fits all" approach, but rather a systematic overview of a variety of tools and techniques. This is not a time management book or a guide to getting organized, nor is it an introduction to conventional project management methodology, nor a review of supervision and delegation techniques. Rather, it is a combination of all these drawn together to examine an under-appreciated aspect of managerial activity— *effectively balancing team efforts to achieve multiple objectives reliably and without undue stress.*

We encourage you to read and think carefully, to draw upon the strategies presented here, and to adapt them to your unique situation. It's not easy to keep several projects on course and successfully completing them. But there are proven ways to do that, and you'll learn about those in this book. As you proceed, we would be very interested in hearing about your experiences, and we encourage you to contact us through our Web site at **www.ducks-in-a-row.com**, or you can also e-mail us at **multiproj@ducks-in-a-row.com**.

Special Features

The idea behind the books in the Briefcase Series is to give you practical information written in a friendly person-to-person style. The chapters are short, deal with tactical issues, and include lots of examples. They also feature numerous sidebars designed to give you different types of specific information. Here's a description of these sidebars and how they're used in this book.

Smart Managing

These boxes are designed to give you tips and tactics that will help you more effectively implement the methods described in this book.

These boxes provide warnings for where things could go wrong when you're trying to organize your workplace to manage multiple projects and responsibilities.

 These boxes highlight insider tips for taking advantage of the practices we describe.

 Every subject has its special jargon and terms. These boxes provide definitions of these concepts.

 It's always important to have examples of what others have done, either well or not so well. Find these stories in these boxes.

 This identifies boxes where you'll find specific procedures you can follow to take advantage of the book's advice.

 How can you make sure you won't make a mistake when managing? You can't, but these boxes will give you practical advice on how to minimize the possibility.

Acknowledgments

First, and deeply, we thank Sarah White, author, consultant, colleague, and friend, for her sage and practical guidance through the process of creating this, our first book. Sarah deserves special credit for keeping us company and keeping us sane through the whole process.

We thank John Woods at CWL Publishing for making this book possible through McGraw-Hill. We also thank Bob Magnan and Nancy Woods, of CWL for the excellent and careful job of editing.

Thanks go to our clients and interviewees who made this book possible by allowing us into their work lives. We particularly appreciate Claudia Vlisides, Rita Garczynski, Beth Stetenfeld, Melissa Sargent, Stacy Sandler, Leslie Cooperband, Joan Gillman, Jane Kinney, and Susan Lehnhardt, who took the time to be interviewed for this effort, and Trip Royal, of Change Directions, for insights on change management.

Our appreciation also goes to Eric Brown, business management consultant and co-chair of Madison Area Business Consultants, for continuing support and encouragement and for volunteering to review the draft.

Deep gratitude to Louis Helling for invaluable support and encouragement.

Finally, special thanks go to our friend, Dan Thompson, who bought the first copy of this book through Amazon.com even before we finished writing it.

About the Authors

Michael Tobis, Ph.D. (systems engineer) and **Irene Tobis**, Ph.D. (psychologist) are partners in the consulting firm Ducks-in-a-Row® Organizing Consultants, a company whose consultations focus on individual and small workgroup operations.

By combining their disparate perspectives and backgrounds, this husband/wife team brings unique insights to its work in individual and group productivity. The give-and-take between Michael's systems engineering approach and Irene's psychological insights has been instrumental in many of Ducks-in-a-Row's successes.

Michael brings an information theory outlook to work process design. With his background in systems engineering, Michael finds questions of prioritization and scheduling particularly interesting.

Irene's background as a psychologist with a focus in stress management underlies her professional activities in workflow consultation. She designs methods tailored to individual skills, resources, styles, and preferences. Her first goal is to get people past feeling overwhelmed. She then proceeds to help clients build skills toward greater productivity and satisfaction.

Manager as Traffic Cop: Managing Multiple Projects

W hat is managing? There's no simple answer to that question. There is, however, a simple reason that there's no simple answer. The role of the manager differs dramatically from one institution or business to another.

There are a few constants, though. You represent a group of people to the world. In a way, you also represent the world to that group of people, so you're in an intermediary position between a working group and the world. On behalf of your working group, you make promises to outsiders. You may also delegate others within the group to make such promises.

In the final analysis, you are held responsible for whether or not those promises are fulfilled.

This book is about making sure the group that you represent can actually do what you've promised, about knowing and remembering what you've promised, and ultimately about fulfilling your promises.

It's your job to know what is going on and what to do about it. You need to be able to see the big picture to get all the puzzle pieces into place.

1

There is much more to managing than this, of course. There are skills in interviewing, hiring, training, and coaching. There are skills in negotiation and compromise. There are skills in finance and marketing. There are skills particular to your line of business. All of these skills are enormously valuable if you keep your promises. However, they won't get you far if you don't.

It's obvious that fulfilling your commitments as a manager is absolutely critical. It's clear enough that keeping track of those commitments is necessary toward fulfilling them. We are constantly surprised that this topic hasn't received a lot of attention.

The manager who can successfully get the most out of the work group has tools for seeing clearly what has been promised and when and by whom it will be delivered. The manager uses that information to ensure follow-through. This book is about the details of that process.

The Missing Tools in the Manager's Toolbox

The manager needs to maintain and study maps of the constantly changing territory in order to navigate effectively. (We'll return to this metaphor occasionally, hopefully without beating it to death.) The skills required to navigate this territory fall between those of *time management* and *project management.* The maps are calendars, tracking tools, and checklists. The vehicle is a coherent, well-thought-out plan that accounts for contingencies. The motive force is a cooperative staff of people who understand the need for this approach.

Usually, people with management responsibilities are responsible not only for their own time, but to some extent, for the allocation of time by the members of the group. This is a more complex problem than conventional time management. It is both an intellectual puzzle and an interpersonal arena. Also, a manager typically has more than one or two major responsibilities. This is even true for a person whose formal title is "project manager" and who holds responsibility for a large, extended project.

The project management literature touches on this intermediate ground in passing, usually with a subchapter on "manag-

Time management The set of skills that individuals develop for allocating their attention across a variety of tasks, obligations, and objectives. The usual tools to accomplish this are a personal calendar and a to-do list.

Project management A well-defined set of skills that are involved in achieving complex objectives involving multiple people, considerable duration, and significant financial commitment. The project manager typically has at most a minor role in designing the project but is responsible for allocating resources within and outside an organization to ensure that the objectives are met on time and within budget.

ing multiple projects," but even so, this tends to refer to a balance of specific, large-scale responsibilities. (See our list of readings in the Appendix to this book for some of our favorites.)

The problem of tracking and fulfilling multiple responsibilities has largely been left to the ingenuity of the individual group leader. Often, managers will solve part of the problem well, while not doing as well on other aspects. There's very little guidance to be found on the skills that are relevant to this problem. We've been working to fill this gap in our consulting work and, now, with this book.

Time Management for Groups and Individuals

One way to look at the problem of your "traffic cop" role, that is, your obligation to effectively allocate the attentions of the group you manage, is to think of it as an elaboration of the time management problem. Conventional time management is about deciding what you are going to do when and then doing it. Group management involves helping the members of the group decide what to do to most effectively achieve the goals of the organization, determining after the fact whether things proceeded according to that plan, and finally making any additional adjustments. In other words, group management is time management on a larger scale, so understanding the hows and whys of personal time management is a prerequisite for effective group management.

Personal Time Management

Time management is a topic that is well covered in many places. Almost everyone who's promoted to manager is exposed to this material. On the other hand, we believe that the skill of crisis management and recovery is a time management topic that hasn't been covered well elsewhere. So, we'll discuss it extensively in Chapter 6.

In this section, we'll review the rudiments of personal time management. We'll draw on these ideas later in the book. If this material is new to you, we urge you to brush up on your personal time management knowledge as soon as you can. Again, see the Appendix for some suggested readings.

Time management is the art of getting the most from yourself in the time available that you can comfortably sustain. You do this by planning, setting up, allocating time, and reviewing.

Planning—Your To-Do List and Your Default Schedule

The professional's most important tool is what was previously known as "the book," a tool that is rapidly being replaced by the personal digital assistant (PDA or palmtop computer). Whether you prefer pen and paper or electronics, you'll find that the four standard PDA features are essential to your life as a manager:

- A personal calendar
- A personal to-do list
- A phone and contact list
- A memo pad

The uses of the phone and contact list and the memo pad are obvious, but using the to-do list and the calendar takes skills that managers need to learn.

The to-do list should be a catchall of any items you decide to address or are even considering. Adding an item to the to-do list is not a time commitment until you move the item to your calendar. Many sources suggest giving each item a priority—a suggestion that we do not support, as we will explain in Chapter 9.

To the extent possible, you should allocate consistent blocks of time to specific aspects of your life. Most people set this up on a weekly basis. Predictable routines, whether washing the car or completing a weekly report, should have particular times of week associated with them, if that's feasible. Even if you can't follow these routines absolutely every week, having a baseline strategy can be very helpful.

Consider, for example, the need to have the oil changed in a vehicle. This requires some effort to keep track of the vehicle mileage (somewhat more difficult with multi-function odometers) and the service history of the vehicle (complicated when there are several vehicles).

Commercial oil-change services support the harried consumer by applying a static-cling reminder to the windshield, showing the mileage of the next required service. Unfortunately, the literal transparency of these stickers often becomes a figurative transparency as well: the sticker becomes so familiar that it stops functioning as a reminder for some people.

There's a simple solution, though. If the sticker isn't reminder enough, put a monthly (or weekly, as fits your driving style) item in your calendar to remind yourself to check whether it's time for an oil change.

The oil-change reminder sticker is an example of two of our favorite principles.

First, it illustrates the advantages of building checks into your routines. It's hard to schedule your next oil change, but it's easy to schedule sufficiently frequent checks as to whether you need one. This moves the oil change from the adrenalin-driven "Oh, my gosh, I have to leave for Chicago in the morning and how long has it been since my last oil change?" to a calm confidence that matters are under control. It may be impossible to make some such maintenance activities routine, but it's possible to make it part of your routine to check on the need for those activities. In general, it's a good idea to check on certain items periodically as a routine, rather than waiting until you feel vaguely uncomfortable about each or all.

MISTAKE PROOFING!
More Impact on Others Than on You

Few people's lives are simple enough that items tacked onto a bulletin board are effective for planning. Often, messages on boards just become clutter. Similarly, other items left about as reminders of tasks become clutter—only too visible to others but virtually invisible to you.

If you don't check visible reminders routinely, they become invisible to you at the times you need them, but are likely to bother you the rest of the time—if you notice them. If you have an effective planning strategy, you don't need visible reminders. If you do not have a strategy, then visible reminders will often fail.

Second, it illustrates how ineffective visible reminders can be. We may leave broken computers in the corner and broken furniture in the hallway, to remind us to replace them or get them repaired, or we may put sticky notes on the wall, to remind us to do something. But those visible reminders may in time become invisible to us—and give visitors and staff the impression that things are disorganized, even frantic. We call this the "invisible corkboard" phenomenon. Almost every corkboard we've ever seen that's used as a personal reminder system has items that are out-of-date and forgotten, items once eagerly and optimistically tacked up, but now history.

Setting Up—Getting Organized

While *being* organized improves efficiency significantly, the activity of *getting* organized can often backfire spectacularly. This is because chronically disorganized people often have accumulated years of material, most of it of little current value.

TRICKS OF THE TRADE
Scheduled Checklists

Gradually build up a list of items that you check weekly, monthly, quarterly, and annually. Each time you complete the checklist, add any generated tasks to your to-do list—and then schedule the next checklist checkup into your calendar.

The worst case is when some small part of it is important. We've seen clients discover large checks or even substantial amounts of cash under piles of junk mail and magazines. But even in such cases, it can take remarkably little time to examine every item to determine whether it's of current importance or not, separating the wheat from the chaff.

The best approach to recovering from chronic disorganization is to start with incoming materials, not with the backlog. The backlog can be quite daunting and time-consuming and it's generally of very little current value.

Organize the Newest First

If you're starting to get organized, you may work up the energy to tackle great piles of unsorted material from past months or even years. This may be therapeutic, but it's counterproductive. Most of that stuff is low priority by now, and there's new material coming in every day.

Start by making sure that you stop adding to your piles. Have systematic ways of dealing with incoming tasks and materials you produce. Don't tackle those piles until you are sure you can keep up with your current flow.

Focus your attention on processing incoming messages, memos, phone calls, e-mails, and letters. Attend to everything while it's current and make sure there's a good place to file it afterwards.

If there are piles that might contain materials of importance, by all means find the time to go through them once—but discipline yourself to process them quickly. Look at each item for exactly one second. Sort the materials into five piles: current business, important archives, trash, route to someone else, and uncertain. The "trash" and "uncertain" piles will probably be the largest. Trash the trash and put the uncertain items into a box and out of the way. Route the routable items, file the archive items, and process the current business into your task management system.

Allocating Time and Reviewing Results

There are many ways to use a personal calendar. One way is simply to list appointments. This is consistent and simple but usually inadequate, because it doesn't link the calendar with the to-do list. Most effective time managers use their calendar to

Stick to One Calendar

Having more than one calendar is a recipe for confusion. If your family needs to see part of your schedule and your staff another, you may need to occasionally update this information. (One of the great advantages of pocket computers is that they facilitate this process.) But it's critical to have a single source that you designate your official calendar. Make commitments only after consulting this calendar. Always record commitments on this calendar.

People who don't follow this advice frequently end up with embarrassing double bookings. People who follow this advice don't.

manage all of their activities, not just their appointments.

The worst approach to time management is to have multiple calendars. Keeping commitments on more than one calendar may make you feel organized, but it's a bad idea because it can lead to confusion.

Allocate your time by transferring activities every week from your to-do list to your calendar. Look through your to-do list and choose items to accomplish in the current week. It can help if your to-dos and your time slots are allocated by category of activity.

Many busy people also do a nightly review and plan for the following day. Making a personal commitment to achieve certain tasks within a day is a good way to make sure you cover all the odds and ends.

The nightly review can also be used for monitoring the effectiveness of your plans. Checking your intentions against your accomplishments and keeping the results in a journal or on your calendar pages can help you identify any problems with your time management. If you're new to this, you may need to accept that this can be embarrassing and frustrating at first, as you identify areas where

Setting an Example

Smart Managing Remember that as a manager you are in a leadership role. If you aren't managing your own time effectively, you'll have great difficulty getting the authority to manage others' time or being a credible model of time management for those around you.

you waste time and procrastinate. There are often emotional aspects to these problems, and some of the time management books can be quite helpful.

The Value of Time Management

It's rare that a manager is unfamiliar with personal time management techniques, but if you are, it's essential that you firmly understand and use effective techniques systematically before you try to implement changes in the activities of your workgroup.

Once you know how to manage your own time and are doing so well enough that you have some extra energy to devote to the big picture, you can begin looking for ways to improve the workflow of your group. As you'll see in later chapters, the approaches build on those of personal time management.

Intuitive Managing and Its Limits

You may find yourself asking, "Do I really need to study how to allocate the group's efforts so carefully?" After all, you've probably encountered managers who don't struggle with these issues. These people always seem to know what to do, always know who to assign to what task, and always get everything done—all without the benefit of much in the way of formal systems.

We've interviewed such people for this book, and they form an interesting contrast with our overwhelmed clients. We've noticed that two features are characteristic of these intuitive managers.

First, they have a central organizing principle for their workflow. For example, we interviewed a long-time school principal who'd been in the same office for many years. The spatial arrangement of his office is very precise and detailed and his weekly schedule regularly moves his attention from one task or area to another. Another manager may rely on daily meetings with the entire staff to maintain a view of what is going on. In every case, the successful manager is expending considerable effort to maintain some sort of a map or model of the enterprise for which he or she is held accountable.

Second, they have been doing their jobs for a long time, and those jobs have been relatively stable. Experience over many years in a consistent environment can lead to an ability to make decisions subconsciously. A person with this sort of experience often has a sense of what to do that is actually the result of many years of successes and failures.

In fact, the intuitive manager can succeed too well. Often-times, the strategy that has emerged gradually as responsibilities have increased reaches scaling limits. In other words, it may happen that responsibilities begin to grow faster than skills improve—until suddenly, things get out of control. At that point, the intuitive method stops working, and the manager needs to make checklists and calendars and new file structures along with the rest of us.

Scaling limits The maximum extent to which a strategy is appropriate for a situation. Applying a strategy to ever larger problems is called "scaling up." At some point in scaling up, most strategies become ineffective; they reach their scaling limits. Take business contacts, for example. A pocket address book is sufficient to a certain point, beyond which a Rolodex® business card wheel works better. Then, as the number of contacts grows, the business may find it necessary to start using file cabinets. When the business reaches a certain size, the bank of file cabinets becomes unwieldy, and it's time to convert to a database program.

It's always wisest to improve a strategy or switch to another before you reach a scaling limit. We all know about the Peter Principle, the theory that employees within an organization will advance to their highest level of competence and then be promoted to and remain at a level at which they are incompetent. In other words, they reach a scaling limit, then pass beyond, only to fail. The way a manager can avoid the problem of scaling limits in terms of his or her time management skills is to keep improving them before it's too late.

> ### An Intuitive Manager with a Scaling Problem
> A client of ours was the founder and executive director of a medium-sized civil engineering firm, with a few dozen professional employees. This company kept all information on a single shared drive on a networked computer. All active projects were set up as subdirectories of a single directory, The CEO, who claimed to be running the company intuitively, admitted to looking at this top-level directory several times a day. This was his map of what his company was doing.
>
> This worked very well until recently. Now, with longer projects and with multiple projects for the same client, the project names are hard to remember and the number of active projects has become so large (about a hundred) that this view is insufficient. Soon, the company will be expanding into a second building, so communication will be less convenient. It's time for this company to consider methods that will scale up to support its larger ambitions.

Contemporary Pressure

In considering these issues of managing multiple projects, which are central to the role of many managers, we find ourselves wondering why so little has been written about managing multiple projects. We can only conclude that these problems were less challenging in the past.

Why has managing multiple projects become more difficult? In the absence of a carefully designed study, we can only speculate.

One possible factor is the trend toward flatter and leaner organizational structures. As a given organization reduces the number of managers, those remaining must assume additional responsibilities.

Another possible factor is that work has become more complex. Companies are increasingly competing on their knowledge and skills rather than on production. This puts more weight on quick thinking, which makes the managerial environment less predictable.

Yet another factor could be that increasing specialization among staff puts pressure on organizations to have more complex interactions among their employees than was formerly the case. The growth of cross-functional activities has changed the traditional structure, dynamics, and culture for managers.

Finally, there's the impact of technology. In the past, most industries and most workgroups had an established lore. These days, things are changing so rapidly that past experience is a less reliable guide. Approaches that our predecessors may have had prescribed are no longer so effective or even applicable. This adds to the number of variables in our problem, making it harder to solve.

Speculation aside, what we see in our work as consultants makes it clear that many managers need to improve their skills at understanding, predicting, and directing the productive activities of their teams.

Multitasking

The world of technology offers a useful concept for managing multiple responsibilities. The word "multitasking" has sometimes been used to mean "doing more than one thing simultaneously," such as reading while exercising or making telephone calls while driving or, perhaps, walking while chewing gum.

The original technical meaning of the term does not refer to actually doing two things simultaneously, though. A computer multitasks by shifting its processing back and forth among various tasks so quickly that it's irrelevant for the user that it's addressing only one at a time. People multitask in this sense as well. When job descriptions call for "effective multitasking", as they often do, they mean that for the purposes of the outside world, the job requires keeping numerous activities moving along. The expectation is for efficient and reliable switching between projects often enough that all of them are addressed effectively, not that a person can write a report with one hand while drawing a diagram with the other.

Workgroups multitask whenever there are more work items to deal with than there are workers to deal with them. To do so effectively requires careful planning. There are no universal recipes for this plan. Planning that may be barely adequate for one group may be excessive and cumbersome for another, and completely off the mark for yet another.

In our role as authors, we can't know as much about your objectives and your resources as we can learn when we consult. There's no one strategy that fits all workplaces. What we can offer you here in this book is a way of thinking about how you can best help your workgroup fulfill its obligations.

> **Multitasking** Making progress on multiple tasks effectively simultaneously by systematically switching between them.
>
> Originally used in the world of computer programming, the term has been extended to people.
>
> A multitasking workgroup makes progress on many fronts and can handle more work items than there are team members. This is possible if there are systematic approaches to making sure that all work items are addressed in sequence.

Our aim is to help you get to a place where your team handles the right number of tasks and gets them done reliably. Our strategy is to help you build maps of the territory. When you make a journey, you need to choose your route and your vehicle and then drive or walk or paddle to get there, but it's much easier to reach your destination with a good map.

Manager's Checklist for Chapter 1

❑ A central part of most managers' jobs is to be the interface between the workgroup and the world regarding the team's work deliveries.

❑ A manager makes promises on behalf of the team and needs to ensure that those promises are fulfilled. Achieving this goal can be complicated in many workplaces.

❑ The tools required to ensure reliable performance of a group fall between those of personal time management and project management in the sense that is used by construction and engineering firms working on very large deliveries.

❑ Many workgroups reach limited success by intuitive and casual methods and find themselves unable to deal with the scale of new opportunities or increased responsibilities.

❑ Workgroups, unlike individuals, are truly "multitasking" in that the group is working on many items simultaneously. (The manager switches between tasks frequently but is only rarely "multitasking".) This is why we work together, but this presents the manager with an ongoing puzzle of how to allocate the team's efforts.

❑ The approaches needed to solve this puzzle build on the techniques of personal time management. An effective manager needs to have good time management skills, both to solve the puzzle and to set a good example for the team.

❑ No book can solve this puzzle for you. This book is intended to help you think clearly about the issues involved in managing multiple projects and find better solutions that match your unique situation.

The Cheeseburger Paradox: The Question of Reliability

Order a Cheeseburger—Get a Cheeseburger

Your local mom 'n' pop restaurant probably serves a meal that's more to your liking than you get at the fast-food franchise down the road. But if you're like most people, you probably find yourself at the franchise as often as not. Why?

The easy answer, of course, is that fast food is faster. Certainly this is part of it, but don't you find yourself saying, "Well, I've only got a half hour and Eb & Flo's *usually* gets the order to me that fast, but I'd better go to Burger Chain just to be sure I'm not late for my appointment"?

Have you ever had the experience of going to a restaurant and having the kitchen totally forget your order? Most of us have experienced this once or twice. This is far more likely to happen at an independent restaurant than at a chain franchise.

This presents something of a paradox. The independent restaurant genuinely cares about your experience. The people working there have a much more personal connection with their employer, so they're also probably motivated to please you. The immediate supervisor is probably better qualified and more highly motivated at the independent than at the franchise. Still, the chain gets you the cheeseburger on time every time and the independent does not!

This paradox doesn't apply just to restaurants. Managers of highly talented groups with wide-ranging responsibilities often find themselves in a similar situation. Things "get dropped." Promises "fall off the table." Opportunities are missed. Customers are dissatisfied. The more highly talented group that prides itself on the highest level of customer service has difficulty meeting the expectations of its customers or constituents. When you forget to respond to a customer, you'll have difficulty convincing them that your service is of a higher quality than the group with simpler responsibilities that gets to everything on time.

The paradox, then, is that the group with more talent is more likely to make mistakes that are visible to the outside world than a competing group with fewer talents.

The reason is fairly obvious—the group with simpler responsibilities has an easier time managing those responsibilities. Notice, though, what this does to the reputation of the more highly skilled group. Your high value added will be weighed against your mistakes. The high-value-added organization can't get by with outperforming the price-point competitor on some features and not on others. The high-value-added organization has to be intensely vigilant to avoid making visible mistakes. Otherwise, the high value won't be perceived and the organization won't thrive. Which, more than likely, is what's happening to Eb & Flo's.

The solutions are less obvious. Eb and Flo have more to think about than the manager of the franchise burger joint across the street, after all. Is it worth it? This book is for the people who think it is. The high-value, high-complexity operation cannot afford to deliver inferior service, even though the added complexity makes such a failure more likely.

Don't Settle for More

It's great to aim high, to attempt to do more and do it better. But unless you can do that reliably, unless your customers can depend on you, you've got problems.

The chain restaurant with the inferior sandwich gets the sandwich to the customer every time. The specialty restaurant may boast better ingredients and preparation, but often the service is sluggish and once in a while the people forget to deliver the order altogether. This is not *despite* their broader talents but *because of* them—they're trying to do more things and so they take on greater complexity.

Complexity is an explanation but not an excuse. The high-value-added operation cannot afford to deliver inferior service.

Managing for Reliability

Unreliable brilliance will almost always lose out to reliable adequacy. Think about that. In most fields, brilliance is worthless without reliability. (A music composer is one of the rare exceptions. A composer can thrive on the results of his or her best efforts, but most of us have to live with the consequences of our failures as well as those of our successes.)

Reliability has a very simple meaning. The reliable worker or workgroup finishes every work item, in a reasonable amount of time and with reasonable quality. Most people who are capable of brilliance are capable of reliability, but it doesn't often come easy. Being competent means you can

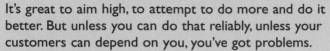

Reliability Getting the job done effectively and on time every time. A reliable individual is capable of being depended upon. The reliable individual has learned to manage peaks and valleys in workload without dropping the ball.

get the job done. Being reliable means you can get the job done every time.

Prioritizing Isn't Enough

Of course, in a crisis situation it's important to prioritize your obligations and decide what to do in what order. In Chapter 6, we'll describe how to recover from an existing work overload.

Key Term   **Workload** The total time that your team will put into a project. It's usually measured in workdays or fractions thereof. Workload may be substantially less than duration if there are points in the project where mechanical processes, outside organizations, or busy queues delay the project while it is active.

Prioritizing your obligations will be an important part of the strategy. And in Chapter 9, we'll go into more detail about the uses and abuses of prioritization.

For the moment, we'll just venture the opinion that prioritization is a wildly over-prescribed medicine, especially if it's not accompanied by other improvements. Many overloaded groups and individuals are forever attending to crises and ignoring other "less important" responsibilities. This is a bad strategy, as responsibilities ignored almost inevitably develop into crises.

Of course, priorities will always exist. Restocking the mailroom should be put on hold if the building is on fire, to take an extreme example. But many people and organizations are far too quick to abandon systematic progress to summon a heroic effort

Focus on Crisis Creates Crisis

For Example   Here's a situation that shows how excessive team focus on crisis causes further crises.

We recently consulted with a very talented and creative new CEO. His strengths were in making deals and in maintaining connections among powerful allies, but he had developed little skill in dealing with details. The CEO, impatient with details, was unresponsive to staff requests for meetings to make decisions that were less than urgent, and he left them hanging regarding which decisions they should make themselves and which they should hand over to the boss.

The natural result was that staff delayed decisions as long as possible, so the office was perpetually in a state of crisis. Things ignored at first because they were not considered urgent would constantly develop into problems. This in turn contributed to the stress that prevented a calm review of pending activity.

We recommended a regular meeting, with administrative staff—and not the CEO—controlling the agenda.

for a particular objective. This strategy should be used very sparingly.

Making Progress on All Fronts

In short, then, always focusing on your high-priority A list until it's completed, and then moving on to the medium-priority B list, is a strategy for a calmer world than you're likely to be facing as a manager. Always focusing on the A list until it's com-

> ### Prioritizing Can Backfire!
>
> **CAUTION!**
>
> An operation that pays attention only to high-priority tasks is constantly generating mini-crises and errors by leaving practically everything to the last minute. Urgent actions and decisions are more stressful than decisions made early. Such stress reduces capabilities, increases peripheral errors, and undermines routines. Focusing on urgent tasks and neglecting those that are not is a great way of making sure you'll have more urgencies than you can handle.

pleted presumes that it will at some time be completed. Always focusing on the A list until it's completed means that items on the B list will languish until they're serious enough to make the A list or are so far overdue that they're best forgotten. Always focusing on the A list is a recipe for permanent crisis.

We need to deliver on every cheeseburger order that we accept, whether or not any single cheeseburger is important to our mission. The reason is simple: although delivering a particular cheeseburger may be unimportant, failing to deliver it is critically important. It affects how we are perceived and the extent to which others will be interested in our services or in cooperating with us.

Your critical objective in managing a complicated work environment is to ensure that every task that's accepted is eventually completed. Everyone who orders a cheeseburger must eventually get one. Also, it must be exactly the cheeseburger that person ordered. What's more, that person must consider the time taken to deliver the cheeseburger to be reasonable.

The basic way to do this is to devote enough time and effort to every task to get it done on time. In practical terms, this

> **If You Can't Possibly Do It, Admit It—Quick!**
>
> If you're starting to fall drastically behind, you can warn your customers about expected delays. In most circumstances, this will slow demand a bit. This will allow you to be honest with the people interested in your work about what they can expect.
>
> The sooner you warn people about impending delays, the better able they will be to adjust. Then, if you succeed in delivering on time, little harm will have been done. On the other hand, if you don't alert anyone to the problem until the last minute, you'll probably cause much greater inconvenience.

means putting time into lower-priority items, even when there are high-priority items on your list!

Strange as it may seem, in the end your best strategy is to spend some fraction of your time dealing with B-list items and, heck, even a C-list item once in a while. We will help you firm up your strategy in later chapters, when we analyze the types of workflow that your group faces and devise strategies that are appropriate for your circumstances.

Keeping All Your Promises

This book will help you manage reliably in the face of complexity. Before we plunge into the details, though, allow us to emphasize the central point. A *commitment is a commitment*. If you can't do something you promised, that's bad. There are no low-priority promises or commitments. When you agree that you or your team will deliver, it's a commitment, not a priority.

Notice that this means two things are necessary. You need to know how available you are for the additional responsibility, and you need to be in a position to refuse it.

If your own boss asks you to do something that's outside your capacity, it's not insubordination to refuse—in fact, it's your responsibility. If the pressure persists, it's best to show the person making the request all of your responsibilities and ask him or her which one to defer or drop. Over-promising to customers or to supervisors is always a bad idea.

Similarly, if a subordinate refuses a request from you, ask

Treat All Commitments as High-Priority Items

The most important factor in being seen as reliable is to deliver on your promises every time. The most important factor in delivering on all your promises is to avoid making promises you can't keep.

Smart Managing

The time to prioritize is *before* you make promises, not *after*. Your overall plan should account for higher- and lower-priority objectives. When someone presents you with a work item and you're deciding whether you can accept it, that's the last chance to consider its priority.

him or her to justify the refusal. (This will help you understand what that person is doing, so there's at least that up side.) If the person's workload is too heavy to allow for the new request, decide which element to defer or drop.

You have the extra duty of repairing any damage caused by this shift, either by transferring some responsibilities to another person or by renegotiating with the person you made your promise to.

This includes commitments to members of your staff. The immediate consequences of failing to meet commitments to your subordinates may be relatively small in the short run, but in the long run not keeping your commitments has enormous consequences in morale, productivity, and even turnover.

Often in a situation of over-commitment, or even of opportunity, internal commitments are the first to go. This almost always appears to be a good short-run solution. In taking this step, it's important to be aware of long-range consequences for morale.

For instance, the result of habitually neglecting an internal process will be that your staff won't take internal process improvements seriously. Not only enthusiasm will suffer. It's also likely that efforts to implement improvements will not meet with enough compliance to put them to the test effectively.

The Intuitive Workplace

You may encounter managers who seem to know exactly what to do next without seeming to plan anything out at all.

An interesting example came up when we did workflow consultations for many of the school principals in our district. Most of them were constantly struggling to keep up with their huge and varied workloads and complex meeting schedules. We applied many of the cognitive techniques that we'll describe in this book and helped them achieve enough visual, spatial, and conceptual clarity that they could be dramatically more effective.

Then we met one fellow who's been principal of a particular middle school for decades. His office is as much a visual jumble as any of the others and his file cabinet is arranged in a fashion we found incomprehensible. He has a cramped and scrawled desktop calendar, with spaces too small to contain all the information he jams into it. Yet, he really does "know where everything is." Though a hard worker (and, like every principal we met, quite willing to do unpaid overtime, an aspect of our school system of which we should not be too proud), this fellow is calmly and contentedly managing while doing almost everything in a way that most people with a much simpler workload would find inadequate. How is this possible?

Without exception, every time we've met a manager who's successfully coping with a complex workload using very simple systems, that person has been in the job for a very long time. The organizational structure that most others would need is burned into that person's mind. That person has become an effective intuitive manager, such as described in Chapter 1.

We've also seen that such managers work in supportive environments. Teachers, staff, parents, and children constantly remind school principals of ongoing problems, and no one wants them to fail or be too quick to take their business elsewhere.

We don't expect many successful intuitive managers to be reading this book. But if you happen to be one, please don't put it aside. There's still the problem of succession. How will you describe your job to your successor when you leave?

Another common feature of the successful intuitive manager is that the workload is more or less constant or has increased gradually over time. Neither situation, by definition, applies to the new manager. Typically, the new manager needs more formality than the person who has been in the position for a long time.

Sometimes the formality that a new manager needs can be temporary; it can be relaxed as the situation becomes more familiar. The new manager may at first require more diligent reporting from the team members, and then may find it possible to loosen the reins.

Even the consistently successful informal workplace may fail abruptly in the face of too much opportunity. According to Dr. Robert Pricer, of the Grainger School of Business at the University of Wisconsin-Madison, about 30% of bankruptcies happen to growing, profitable businesses. The immediate cause is always a cash-flow crunch, but this can be seen as lack of foresight, as managers doing things the way they've always been done and relying on a sense that "things are all right" rather than doing a cash flow analysis, which is a very boring exercise in a steady company but absolutely critical in one undergoing rapid growth.

An Intuitive Manager: Groundskeeper at a Fortune 500 Headquarters

We know of a facilities supervisor for the national head-quarters of an insurance company. Managing four employees, she's responsible for maintaining an enormous complex of hundreds of acres, including highly landscaped displays, a prairie restoration, and a great deal of road and parking space. She's also started and continues to manage several recycling programs.

In the Wisconsin climate, the nature of the work varies dramatically with the seasons. This manager was trained as a landscape architect and never received any management training. Her only formal technique is to "write things down on a pad of paper and cross them off when they are done." Yet, she manages all this complexity quite successfully. She fits our profile of the successful intuitive manager: she's been at the job a long time and her responsibilities have grown gradually along with the size of the company and properties.

But there's a problem. She is approaching retirement. She speculates that when she leaves no one will be able to fill her role and the company might outsource its landscaping needs to a specialized company.

Many problems of organization are scale-dependent. If you have five pieces of paper to keep track of, it's reasonable to just stack them on your desk. If you have five thousand, you need a file cabinet and a firm grasp of the alphabet. If you're running the Library of Congress, you need something considerably more complicated than that. If you're a freelance writer, you can handle your business with a to-do list. If you're the CEO of General Electric, it takes something more complicated than a simple to-do list.

Manager's Checklist for Chapter 2

❑ Reliability is part of value. High-value-added operations are more challenging to manage and are more likely to have reliability problems than simpler operations. This detracts from their perceived value and hurts them in the marketplace.

❑ The value of prioritization is overstated and prioritization is misused. You should prioritize *before* you make a commitment, not *after*. To be perceived as reliable, you must treat every commitment as a high priority.

❑ Habitual prioritization of ongoing tasks leads to a crisis mentality. This in turn leads to frequent crises.

❑ Time must be allocated to every commitment. The time allocation needs to be careful and consistent.

❑ Tracking workloads is a necessity in a busy workplace. When a workload becomes excessive, it's necessary to renegotiate, but this should be avoided as much as possible.

❑ Some workplaces can get by informally. These are usually places with long-term stability, limited growth rates, and tight integration with other groups that tend to catch errors early in a supportive way.

The Formal Workplace and Its Forms

M ost people enjoy working in an organized workplace, but many of the same people detest filling out forms. The similarity among the words "form," "formal," and "information" is not coincidental, since the words originate from the same root. In many situations, enforcing forms is an essential part of the formalism that a workgroup needs to get the information that's in its forms to the people who need it. In fact, one of those people who need the information could be you.

Unfortunately, it's not a simple tradeoff. The workplace with insufficient information collection may be disorganized, but the workplace with too many forms may be disorganized as well. The formalism needs to be appropriate and adequate to the task, but not excessive. In this chapter we consider how and why.

Why Formalize?

Formalizing a workplace makes it into a system, which can be better understood and controlled. In essence, you're giving up some freedom to make the workplace more effective.

The Formal Workplace

The extreme of high formality occurs in many situations, but it's consistently present in two sorts of settings.

Formality emerges in high-stakes industries, such as aviation, medicine, banking, and finance. In fields like these, mistakes can have enormous consequences. Formality is required and enforced. Here's an example. An airline pilot has a very specific checklist that needs to be completed in a very specific sequence before any flight can take off. No matter how skilled and confident the pilot may be, the checklist remains a legal requirement.

The other case of extremely formal management is in high-volume, low-margin commodity industries. This brings us back to our burger chain example. The chain may claim in its marketing that you can have it your own way, but there are a limited number of choices available to the customer. The reason for this is to reduce the number of decisions the production staff has to make, ideally to no decisions at all. The ideal day at a franchise restaurant is one where no member of the staff is confronted with any decisions at all!

In the case of the pilot, it's a matter of life and death. You really don't want the pilot cutting corners on the checklist any more than the FAA does, do you? In the case of the burger joint, it's simply a matter of holding on to a narrow profit on a large number of small transactions.

It's very interesting to note the common thread here. Systems become more formal when they are less tolerant of error. In other words, the formal system is much more reliable than the seat-of-the-pants method.

How It Works—Creative Constraints

Formalism can be defined as a set of mandated constraints on behavior. In this way, business and workplace formalism is like local law. Formalism has the advantages and the disadvantages of law. By restricting certain options, it enables other options.

Consider the law that you have to drive on the right side of the road. This reduces by half the amount of pavement available to you. Most people don't regard this as an onerous constraint, because general acceptance of this rule makes it possible to drive much more rapidly on the half of the pavement that remains available.

Formalism at the burger joint reduces the cost of production and increases reliability. By constraining the employees quite rigorously, it's relatively easy to train for their jobs and therefore those jobs are available to people with limited skills.

Formalism in the cockpit reduces the chance of error and builds in checks of safety systems in a way that a more casual safety checkup might miss.

How to Formalize with Forms

Let's recall our basic purpose here. We can borrow the watchword of project management, which exhorts you to "complete your work on time, on spec, and under budget." In order to achieve this daunting goal, we seek sufficient control of our processes.

Control Theory

There's a body of engineering knowledge called "control theory" that refers specifically to the control of complex systems. (It used to go by the name "cybernetics," but that word was much misused and eventually abandoned by engineering professionals.) The mathematics can get quite complicated in some situations, but the basic ideas of control theory are simple.

The components of a control system (and how this applies to the situation of a front-line manager) are:

1. A system being controlled (the work of

> **Key Term**
>
> **Control theory** A branch of engineering that describes strategies for controlling complex systems. Control theory is based on the principle of feedback. It compares the actual and intended state of a system, and takes corrective action based on the measure of the difference and estimates of the delay in the system's responses to inputs. Control theory teaches managers to use models, measurements, and reports to analyze and improve complex systems.

your workgroup) and a desired state of the system (a calendar of work product expectations).

2. A simplified model of the system, so that you can effectively analyze it (the business and workplace rules that are in place to make the work manageable).

3. Measurements of the current state of the system (raw data you collect from talking to the troops or formalized information collected from them or their tools).

4. A way to calculate how far you are from the desired state (collated and processed information).

5. Ways to steer the system back to the desired state (systems for controlling behavior, mostly your power to delegate various assignments in various ways).

The strategy of steering a system to its desired condition based on its difference from a predetermined objective is called "feedback control" and the difference from the ideal state is called the "feedback."

> **Key Term** **Feedback** The measure of how far a system is from a desired state. The use of that measurement to enhance the system behavior is called *feedback control*.

Feedback can be misused. The worst case is steering the system to increase the feedback signal rather than to decrease it. Here's an example with which you're most likely familiar. Sometimes the volume on microphones or electric guitars works too well: the sound is amplified by the speakers, passes through the microphone, and is further amplified, over and over, resulting in a loud whine or other sonic distortion. Turning the volume down solves the problem. This is called "unstable feedback" and it's not a good way to run a business.

The Purposes of Forms

The main ingredient of a control strategy is information.

There are two ways a manager can get the information needed to control the system: informal interview and formal

measurement. The more ambitious manager needs a component of formal measurement to accomplish the job at hand.

The traditional way to gather formal information is by filling
out a form at certain points in the work process. Because of the
need for information, a lot of forms show up in our daily lives.
These include time sheets, expense accounting forms, subscrip-
tion forms, purchase orders, and telephone message pads. This
information is collected and collated in various ways, often by
clerical workers filling out additional forms. (Of course, where
it's practical to computerize the form-filling, this greatly facili-
tates collating the information.)

Another way to use forms is to provide a view of the information. Forms of this type require no additional processing.

Your personal calendar is in this category. Another example
is a status check. When there's a set of tasks to be performed,
the cross-shift handoff can be greatly facilitated by the expedient of having a list of items to check off: the second shift can
take over where the first shift ended if the first shift has clear
ways of indicating what work it has done. Your accountant is
familiar with the balance sheet, profit/loss statements, and cash
flow analyses, for example. These forms provide dramatically
different views of the business and each serves a different purpose. Similarly, in managing multiple projects, you'll probably
wish to construct a project view, to show the status of each
project as a function of time, and an assignment calendar to
show which staff is on which project when. Gantt and PERT
charts are well-known forms that provide views of project information. (We'll say more about the various ways to view your
information in later chapters.)

Another way that forms can be helpful is to implement useful constraints.

An example of a useful constraint is the cash register at a
fast food restaurant, which has items, rather than numbers on it.
The idea is that fast food checkout staff are not qualified to set
prices on custom sales.

A form that provides a useful constraint is a safety checklist.

The employees maintaining boats at a resort may need to check every item on a list. The form itself contains little information—typically every completed form looks the same. The form serves as a method to constrain the behavior in the desired pattern.

Resistance

Regardless of the value of forms to you as a manager, your employees will generally not enjoy filling them out and will tend to resist. This is especially true if you introduce new forms. Even if it doesn't take much time to fill out a form, it's regarded as an extra task. Most workers do not consider providing information about their work production to be a part of their production, even if you as a manager do.

If you need additional information, look for creative ways to get it. Add a line or two to an existing form, if you can. If you need to add a new form, see if there's an old one that can be eliminated at the same time, to minimize the number of forms to keep track of.

Invest some time in the aesthetic layout of the form. U.S. government agencies set stunningly bad examples for form design. (Other countries do better.)

Many computer companies, including Microsoft and Apple, do a good job with the design of on-screen computer forms. When the forms ask for input, they use features with similar shapes for information of similar types, indicating the sort of information (check box, selection, text) elicited.

The use of colored paper can also be surprisingly helpful. The color might make a form a bit easier on the eyes, but, more important, it makes the process easier to remember. It's far easier to remember the correct context for using "the blue form" or "the yellow form" than it is for using a Form WX254 or a WZ245.

> **TRICKS OF THE TRADE**
>
> ### Colorful Forms
>
> Pay attention to having a pleasant and clear layout for your internal forms. Use a different paper color for each. The paper colors will help people associate each information task with the part of the workflow where it's required.

Form Portfolio

If your operation uses a variety of forms, keep a notebook with one copy of every form. With each form, keep a record of the date and quantity printed and when it was last revised. Every time you think of a change to be made to that form, open the appropriate section of the notebook and make a note of it. When it's time to reorder, you'll have all the information you need in one place.

The form portfolio makes it easy to keep your forms current and evolving. It's also easy to use this history to identify forms that go out of use as operations change. If a form is in disuse, it's time to re-examine that aspect of your procedures. Has that activity become so marginal that it should be abandoned? Or is there a lack of compliance with the policy? Keeping a forms portfolio can help you identify such issues.

In the end, though, you need to draw on your motivational skills. Explain to your staff why information is central to your mission and ask them to realistically estimate how much time a form will take once they've become familiar with it.

The Best Way to Avoid Forms

A major advantage of information technology is that it can collect information at the same time it is distributing it. Whether or not your staff has desk jobs, they are all probably working with some sort of machine with computer technology in it.

Since most people like to do their jobs but most dislike reporting on them, it's a great advantage if you can find ways to enforce reporting and yet make it as unobtrusive as possible. Many manufacturers of workplace tools have come to understand this and have built reporting features into their devices. In the excitement of bringing new equipment or software on line, it may not seem timely to understand the reporting features. However, taking the time to do so immediately will make your information more reliable while simultaneously reducing the workload of the machine's users.

Bad Formalism (Bureaucracy)

Formalism isn't easy, though. You probably don't have the resources of the Federal Aviation Administration or McDonald's Corporation at your disposal. That being the case, you should introduce formalism carefully. (In later chapters we'll have things to say about the process of changing to a new system.)

There's certainly a lot of bad formalism. It's often called "bureaucracy"—a word that's typically uttered with an unmistakable tone of contempt. We retreat to the term "administration" as neutral, and we bow to the majority in treating the word "bureaucracy" as indicating problems. It gets in the way of managing multiple projects even as formalism helps.

Almost everyone has stories of some of the excesses of bureaucracy. Since we're at risk of promoting bureaucracy simply by advocating formality in the workplace, we think it's worthwhile to take a look at how bad formalism occurs.

> **Key Term**
>
> **Bureaucracy** Peter Scholtes, in his book, *The Leader's Handbook*, defines "bureaucracy" as "unuseful constraint." Scholtes follows this with a delightful exercise in sarcasm from the Napoleonic wars, in which the Duke of Wellington, in hot pursuit of Napoleon, found himself also the recipient of quibbling queries regarding details of his inventory. Wellington, writing his response to the authorities in London, admits to a "hideous confusion as to the number of jars of raspberry jam" and asks whether his mission is to "train an army of uniformed British clerks ... or ... to see to it that the forces of Napoleon are driven out of Spain."

There are at least three main flavors of bad formalism:

- Invoking a rule that doesn't apply
- Applying the wrong rule
- Rules that serve no purpose

We'll talk about each.

Invoking a Rule That Doesn't Apply

One type of bad formalism is the ill-specified constraint. This is the case where the rules are clear and straightforward—but obviously wrong.

As an engineering graduate student in the early days of the cheap computer-on-a-chip, one of us (Michael) was in a project-based class whose intent was to take an off-the-shelf computer chip and wire it and program it to read and write data to a disk.

"We had the disk, the wires, the resistors and capacitors and other small parts, the manuals, and the power supply," he says. "The computer chip, however, did not arrive until finals week. Everyone in the class got an 'A.' (Now it can be told—this is part of his GPA!)."

Why did this $80 part cause a dozen University of Florida graduate students to waste three units of tuition? At the time (1976), it was inconceivable to the university system that a "computer" could be a casual purchase. The purchase of a computer had to be approved by the state government in Tallahassee. They did manage to expedite the purchase so that we eventually received the device and a couple of the more ambitious students managed to get the little green light on the disk drive to blink.

In this case the rule was wrongly invoked. Had someone made the decision early on that "this rule was obviously not intended to apply to this situation," there would likely have been no consequence. Instead, several credits were handed out for no reason and time and money were wasted.

> **Inappropriate Application of a Rule**   Smart Managing
>
> An $80 part required on short notice took months to deliver because someone in purchasing decided that the purchase was covered by a rule that was intended for much more expensive systems.
>
> Every rule has marginal cases. If a situation is a judgment call, where it might not really make sense to apply the rule, it may be better to take the risk of cutting corners than to take the certain cost of overly complex requirements.

Applying the Wrong Rule

Another bureaucratic problem is diligent application of the wrong rule.

This is the most typical cause of misfiling in an office. Consider the business that has the IRS as a customer. How does it ensure that the client files don't get mixed up with the tax files?

A good example of "wrong rule" bureaucracy happened to a friend who got a job as a scientist at a major federal laboratory. Upon arriving at his newly assigned office, he found a desk and a computer, but no chair. He asked around about getting a chair and was eventually directed to the purchasing agent for the division, who acknowledged his request and promised that a chair would be delivered soon. This left our friend still standing, so he snuck into a conference room and borrowed a chair for what he expected would be a few hours, perhaps a day or two.

Months passed. Our friend, still sitting on the borrowed chair, had completely forgotten the incident, when a brand new, shrink-wrapped office chair arrived in the office.

In this example, the purchasing agent misunderstood the problem or chose to do so. He received a reasonable request and discharged his duty as a purchasing agent: he purchased something. He did not take the time or trouble to note that this purchase was not the right solution to the actual problem.

Whether there was a more appropriate procedure for getting a chair for an office, our friend never knew. By that time, though, he was sufficiently acculturated to know that disposing of a borrowed chair could be as problematic as acquiring one, so he finished his tenure at the laboratory with two chairs.

Rules That Serve No Purpose

Yet another type of bureaucracy is the "leftover" system. In these cases, a constraint has been put in place to resolve a problem that is no longer present or that has been resolved by some other means.

Here's an example from our experience. A business with a complicated procedure for scheduling personnel in the field scaled back, leaving only the founder doing fieldwork. The founder, nevertheless, habitually filled out two calendars and a checklist so that everyone's calendar would be up-to-date. This went on for some time before he realized that the extra work was something he had put in place so that others would be informing him and each other of their availability. Those others no longer existed, so the procedure was slowing things down while achieving nothing!

Peter Scholtes offers the rather portentous word "skeuomorph" for this phenomenon. The term, used in archeology, denotes an activity or a feature that continues in use long after its original purpose disappears. It's an impressive word, but less commonly used than the more casual "cruft."

That's the term used in the world of computer programming. Cruft refers to computer code that is still part of a distributed product although it no longer serves any purpose and, in some cases, may cause the product to operate less

> **Cruft** A casual term for procedures that are still in place but serve no purpose and take time and effort.
>
> An example of cruft is performing complex schedule synchronization procedures in a business that has scaled back to one field employee.

efficiently. Cruft can eventually become a significant debugging and maintenance problem.

The term cruft no longer applies just to problems of superfluous code. It also more generally denotes procedural steps that no longer serve a purpose. A new machine on a factory floor may maintain a production count, even as the worker diligently continues to keep track with pencil and paper. Because no one told the operator that it was no longer necessary to track production manually, the activity continues, as cruft.

The Common Thread of Bureaucracy

The point that all of these examples have in common is clear. The problem is not the existence of a rule. The problem is the inappropriate application of a rule.

Such cases are unavoidable. Rules are not rules if they are too easy to bend or to change. Consequently, sometimes rules will be applied inappropriately. The problems of bureaucracy arise when rules are so inflexible that they don't fit the realities of the situations and people don't take them seriously. The problems arising from informality come from rules being so flexible that people don't take them seriously.

The Worst of Both Worlds

Many a workplace struggles with the tradeoffs between formalism and informality. Often this ends up as a power struggle between the free spirit (or "unreliable") person and the rational (or "micromanaging") person. The tradeoffs should be made carefully and with attention to the right balance. Simply writing it off to "win some, lose some" can lead to the worst of both worlds—you may bear the burden of formalism with none of its benefits.

An example occurred in a small business we know, where a public vacation calendar had been implemented but not adequately explained to everyone. The problem arose when one employee marked himself on vacation on the calendar, while the designated backup to the first employee, who was unaware of the new system, simply asked his supervisor for permission to take off. The end result was not only that the job was left uncovered for a few days, but also that all the work that went into designing the new system was in vain.

When you implement a formalism, schedule time to review whether it's achieving its purpose and to improve or abandon it as appropriate.

If You Pay the Price, Get the Benefits

When you implement a formalism, do so thoroughly and set a time to review its success. Otherwise, you may end up in a situation where people are paying the costs of the formalism but not realizing the benefits. This is poor management, with lasting results: people disappointed or frustrated by the experience will be less supportive of subsequent attempts to implement formalisms.

Worthwhile Constraints

Now that we know what to watch out for, let's consider what we're aiming at. What are the advantages of a well-designed formalism?

The one that most easily comes to mind is quality control. That's the purpose of the formalism at both the airline and the burger chain. If an organization constrains behavior in certain ways, it eliminates the most common forms of error, one by one. For the smaller sorts of operations that concern us here, this level of detail is not attainable. A typical manager doesn't have the sample size to identify every type of error that is likely to arise.

Still, this sort of formalism is crucial to our main objective— reliability. In order to keep every promise, there has to be some way to keep track of every promise. The basic design of our system has to be that progress is made on every work item in a timely fashion.

There is a second advantage, at least as important in many managerial situations—communicating to the manager exactly what's going on in the manager's domain.

In order for us to make effective decisions as managers, we need current and accurate information about the state of the operation. The informal way to achieve this is to maximize the amount of time spent in meetings with staff. However, such meetings are costly. In most work environments, much of the burden of the managerial meeting can be transferred to formal reporting procedures.

This aspect of formalization we call the *creation of views*. A view is a big-picture representation of your operation or some aspect of it.

A view is impossible without the data to construct the view. Yet another purpose of formalism, besides directly constraining the processes you manage, is to allow you to observe and control those processes.

Whatever the critical questions that determine the health of

Key Term **View** A big-picture representation of an aspect of an operation or project. Since the workplace is multi-dimensional, there are multiple ways of looking at it. To look at finances, for example, you could use a balance sheet, a profit/loss statement, or a cash flow analysis: each provides a very different view of the financial realities, for different purposes. To look at projects, you could use Gantt charts, PERT charts, and work breakdown structure charts: each presents information for a different view.

your operation, you should devise a view of the relevant parameters. Then, you need to decide how those parameters should be measured. Finally, you need to put those measurements in place.

Note that these measurements constitute a real overhead for your staff, and a perceived overhead that, for some reason, generally seems to be larger than the actual overhead. Your requests for information may cause some friction between you and those who report to you. You will need to make the case that the measurements you're taking will be worth the extra effort because they will enable the entire organization to make better decisions ... and make decisions better.

The Happy Medium

Tom DeMarco is the author of several fascinating books on software engineering management. His focus is on stimulating creativity in a profession that has a reputation for being drudgery, but where success depends largely on bursts of intense creativity and close cooperation. DeMarco has become a sworn enemy of excessive formalism in the engineering environment. His argument is that systematizing and compartmentalizing creative work dramatically reduces the possibility for unexpected connections and surprising collaborations.

Even the best-designed formalism is a system of constraints. If your product is an unprecedented piece of design or technology, you may wish to tread very lightly regarding how formal the workplace will be for your most creative staff.

We urge you to keep this tradeoff in mind as you go through the detailed recommendations in the following chapters. Excessive formalism can be just as bad for a business as inadequate formalism—and an abrupt switch from one to the other is frequently worst of all.

Finding the happy medium isn't a simple matter. Just because a group is intermediate in formalism doesn't mean it's found the happy medium. It's possible, especially in groups where there's been some tension over the optimal degree of formalism, to find that some things that should be formalized are casual and other things that should be casual are overly formalized! Where hair-splitters have been in a tug-of-war with seat-of-the-pants types, the results may carry scars from the process.

That's a tricky situation to repair, since the ideal is to remove some formalisms and add others.

In the end, though, the measure of success is intuitive. The right system "feels right." Your clue is your gut feeling whether you can get a grip on things or not. If you understand what's going on but aren't drowning in detail and your staff doesn't feel that your efforts to understand interfere with their work, you're getting it right.

Walk the Talk

If you succeed in finding the happy medium, remember that it still amounts to constraining the behavior of your staff. Don't let yourself off the hook. If you implement time sheets, fill one out yourself. If vacations for staff now require a four-week lead time, don't just take off for a day. It's about more than being a role model for your employees; it's about knowing how the constraints feel.

Successful formalization can reap great rewards, but unsuccessful efforts can be worse than no effort at all. Effort invested in planning and implementation will have been wasted and the procedures after such a failure tend to remain muddled for some time. When you add a system, stick to it rigorously. If there are constraints on your staff, apply them to yourself as well.

Manager's Checklist for Chapter 3

❑ The most reliable workplaces are highly formal, but not all highly formal workplaces are reliable. Formal systems need to be done right.

❑ Formalizing a workplace makes it into a specified system, which can be better understood and controlled.

❑ Formalizing a workplace trades some freedom for greater effectiveness.

❑ Systems are controlled by comparing an ideal state with an actual state, which requires measurements. Often, the way to measure your workgroup's performance is to implement forms for staff to fill out at certain points in the workflow. Most people find forms unpleasant, so make sure that your forms are minimally intrusive and as easy as possible to work with.

❑ If possible, find ways to do your tracking unobtrusively, by measuring the output from the tools your staff is using.

❑ Badly designed or out-of-date formalisms can be worse than no system at all. Formalize carefully. Follow through. Obey your own rules scrupulously.

Taskonomy: Categorizing Your Work

Why Categorize Work?

Planning workflow is the dominant activity of a manager in many workplaces and is an important part of managing multiple projects. This amounts to constantly bringing together three items—a time, a person, and a task. The person performing the task needs to be able to focus on the work and may rely on you to identify the work that is going to get done.

Keeping a complicated workgroup on track is no picnic. You need to know what's been promised for when and what's brewing. You need to know what needs to be done and who's good at what. You need to know who can do what and who's doing what and who's doing something you've never heard about. You need to know how busy everyone is and when anyone is available. You need to know what's in jeopardy and what's on target. You need to know not only what you need to do next, but also what everyone else needs to do next. Then you have to make sure that it gets done.

We begin by considering the various types of work and how they relate to one another.

The word "taxonomy" refers to the way biologists categorize all life into species, genus, and so on. We've coined the word "taskonomy" for our purpose here. We're trying to classify the types of work. This will help us lay out strategies, in subsequent chapters, for getting the project work done.

Our goal is to put together a big picture of the responsibilities of your workgroup. A big picture can be put together from jigsaw pieces. This is a sort of bottom-up approach. Many management books and courses start at the top, at a strategic or even a philosophical level, but we start with the pieces.

Many management situations begin with the manager having a problem of "can't see the forest for the trees." (OK, that's mixing metaphors a bit. Let's imagine a jigsaw puzzle of a forest scene! The analogy works out nicely—you open the box and can't see the forest, but you have a lot of tiny odd-shaped pictures of trees.)

In this chapter we're aiming for clarity on the pieces that make up the puzzle. We're going to be a bit fussy about definitions here, and we'll be using certain words more specifically than they might be used in casual conversation.

One reason for this is that some types of work are mutually incompatible. You may wish to separate these in time or assign them to separate people. We'll be identifying these as we go. In the jigsaw analogy, these would be pieces that look like they might fit together, but really don't quite.

The bigger purpose also has a jigsaw analogy. The first step to solving a jigsaw puzzle is to gather similarly colored pieces together. The big picture will gradually emerge. We'll be working toward the big picture of your workgroup's responsibilities by completing the project they have been assigned, but we'll take the road less traveled and start at the bottom.

Tasks: What Are They?

All work is made up of tasks and only of tasks. That's simple enough. But what's a task?

We use the word "task" in a very specific way. By "task" we

mean the atomic unit of work. This doesn't refer to nuclear physics. We mean that a task is the fundamental unit, the smallest component of work that is useful for planning purposes.

Since we are human beings, we sleep every night. Only a fraction of our day is devoted to the workplace. Of course this is obvious, but it has very real implications for how we structure our work. The fact that we need to sleep means that there's a fundamental unit of work that cannot exceed an entire workday. After that period of time, there's a biologically mandated break in the work. Even if a person has an objective to complete that will span several days, it's necessary to find breaking points in that objective.

> **Task** For our purposes, a unit of work that can in principle be undertaken by a single person without interruption. A task must therefore take less than a single workday.

More typically, we take on several tasks a day. The number depends on the type of work. A receptionist may have many dozens of small work items to handle in a day, while an engineer counts it as a good day if nothing draws his or her attention away from the project that's the main focus and so, from our point of view, may have only one task. Now, if that engineer has a meeting in the middle of the day and two sessions of concentrated design work, even though both of those sessions may be directed toward the same goal, they must be considered as two tasks. It's necessary to find a good stopping point twice in that day.

Now that we've established that a task has a maximum duration of a workday, let's consider its minimum duration. To type this paragraph, I needed to

> **Duration** The amount of time from its inception to its completion, usually measured in clock hours or calendar days.

compose several sentences. Was each one a task? Each sentence comprised several words. Was each a task? Each word consists of one or more letters. Was each a task? Shall I consider it a task to end this paragraph with this question mark?

The Trash Task—or Not?

Is taking out the garbage a task?

In a typical household, it is a task, though it may involve dealing with several trash bins. It might be handled informally: whichever member of the household encounters a full bin takes the trash outside.

At a large restaurant, it is a daily chore with several steps. A well-run restaurant will assign the various steps to particular people on each shift in a systematic way. In that case, it constitutes several tasks.

At a corporate headquarters or other large facility, taking the garbage out is a serious matter, which requires careful planning and management to ensure that it's done correctly. There, "taking out the garbage" is a significant enterprise that may have frequent contingencies and significant planning involved.

Whether a work item is a task or not depends on context.

Here, we need to keep an eye on our purpose. We're trying to determine how our group should allocate its attention. Composing a certain amount of text is reasonably a task for planning purposes, provided that the person producing it can do so in a single uninterrupted work period.

Why It Matters—Stopping Points

To an individual worker managing his or her own workload, the boundary where one task lets off and another picks up is important. The task boundary is a natural stopping point or breaking point. As an extreme example, you don't want your receptionist abandoning a telephone conversation with a client! If the receptionist needs a break, it's much better to have that break between calls.

Almost all forms of work have natural stopping points, though they may be less obvious than hanging up at the end of a phone call. A good stopping point is one where a phase is completed and another is about to start. A good stopping point separates two work items that are usefully distinguished for planning purposes.

Stopping points are important because, like a computer, a person needs to "boot up" into a given task. Some tasks are easier than others. Answering the telephone takes an instant,

The Tasks of Proposal Writing

Writing a proposal is a sequence of tasks.

If you're responding to a significant request for proposals, it's unlikely that you'll be able to complete it in one sitting. Even if this is entirely your responsibility, you likely break it up into task units. By promising yourself a coffee break as soon as you've written the next section, for example, you're doing task-based planning. Note also that pausing at the end of a complicated section, say a budget spreadsheet or a timeline, is much more efficient than stopping in the middle. The cost of "Now, what was I thinking?" may be significant.

but other tasks take some time to restart the thinking process. It depends on the nature of the task. Answering a ringing telephone takes very little time, but initiating a call may take more. Some tasks may involve spreading out the paperwork, reviewing what you were doing last time, and figuring out what the next step is before any forward progress is possible.

Why It Matters—Handoffs

Often in the course of a project, a sequence of tasks will be passed from one worker to another. In this case, a clear definition of the boundary between tasks can be very valuable. We see this process causing difficulty so often for our clients that we've given it a name: the baton-passing problem.

In a relay race, one athlete hands off the baton to the next. No matter how each athlete performs individually, an awkward handoff can keep the team from performing up to its potential. In many workflow situations, this handoff can be muddied. One of the most common causes of unreliability in a workgroup process is a poor handoff of a task.

Sometimes a person completing a work phase will e-mail the results to another, who may imagine it as a work in progress and may not understand that the handoff is complete. This often occurs because both parties have not agreed on the boundary between tasks, with one seeing the work as complete and the next seeing it otherwise.

Sometimes a person completing a step will pass it along to

a manager, at which point a simple miscommunication disrupts the process. The manager believes that the worker will pass the product along to the next worker, while the worker believes that the manager will take care of the handoff.

Sometimes a person who rarely uses e-mail will drop something into the mail slot of a person who rarely receives paper mail or a person will e-mail information to a person who's expecting the information to come in the form of a memo.

You rarely see a track team lose the baton altogether, but it's amazingly common in business! Here's how we suggest handling this problem: don't treat the handoff as a separate task. Treat the handoff as the deliverable from the task. That is, if Alice is developing some film and Bob is making a print (the next phase), Alice's task is not defined as "develop the film" or even as "develop the film and give it to Bob," which sounds like two tasks, but

> **⚠ CAUTION!**
>
> **Don't Drop the Baton!**
>
> The nitty-gritty of teamwork often involves passing work from one pair of hands to another. Be sure that this handoff is clear. Define the point at which the task is complete and define to whom the task is handed off and how.
>
> It's usually clearest to include the handoff as part of the task, so it's the responsibility of the person completing a phase to ensure that the next person in the chain receives the results.

"give the developed film to Bob." The responsibility for the handoff not only goes to the first person in the sequence, but that responsibility is expressed as the whole task. After all, Alice can't give developed film to Bob if the film isn't developed.

Sequences and Sets of Tasks

In order to talk specifically about work, we need to share a specific vocabulary. The box starting on the next page provides definitions of terms we'll use throughout the rest of this book.

All work can be broken down into tasks. This can happen in an enormous variety of ways.

Task A task is a unit of work that can in principle be undertaken by a single person without interruption. A task must therefore take less than a single workday.

Work process A work process refers to any set of one or more tasks that achieves a particular objective.

Workload The workload of a work process, as used here, refers to the total number of hours that the team spends on a particular work process. For planning purposes, this is often an estimated workload.

Thread A thread is a sequence of tasks set up in such a way that the completion of one work item kicks off the start of exactly one more item or ends the thread. The tasks are like beads on the thread. Each bead, except the start bead and end bead, has a predecessor and a successor.

One-off A one-off task refers to a task that is not started by the completion of one or more tasks and does not cause the start of one or more tasks. A one-off task is not part of any thread.

Multithreading Multithreaded work processes are ones designed such that different parts of the work occur simultaneously. This approach, when feasible, reduces the total duration of a project, but increases other costs.

Project A project is a work process with a definite end product and a target closing date. For many high-value-added organizations, project work is the product, the way to satisfy the customer or end user.

Routine A routine is a work process that is ongoing. There is no desire or expectation that such work will end. It often has the characteristic of maintenance or support of the organization.

Cyclic work Cyclic work refers to an aggregation of projects and routines at a workplace where the workload is highly dependent on season.

Background work Background work is work that is neither routine (required maintenance) nor project-driven (required delivery date). This is work that is productive toward some long-range goals but isn't urgent, and is used to fill in times when there are no immediate demands on which progress can be made.

To be clear, we'll call any set of tasks intended to serve some business goal a work process. In the remainder of this chapter, we consider the more important ways in which a work process can be made up of tasks.

One-Off Tasks

The simplest case is a one-off task. This is the rare case of a single action that is required of a single person that does not start, continue, or end any larger work item.

A memo that you receive and read but that requires no action from you is a one-off task. Others may be more in the target audience ("persons wishing to take Columbus Day off need to put in their requests by October 1") and may need to do something else (to protect their holiday plans). For those persons, the memo creates a mini-project, deadline and all.

Threads

Any work that is not in the one-off category consists of at least one thread. We borrow this term from computer programming. To a programmer, a thread is a sequence of tasks that is assigned to a single processing chip. To us, it's simply a sequence of tasks such that the completion of any one (except the last one) causes another task to begin.

Each work process consists of at least one thread, but it may contain several threads. In general, different people can be assigned to the different threads.

For example, if you're baking cornbread alone, there's only one thread. You mix the wet ingredients. You mix the dry ingredients. You fold them together. You pour the batter into a baking pan. You bake it. If you have company in the kitchen, you can multithread the project. You can ask your companion to measure and mix the dry ingredients while you measure and mix the wet ones. At that time, a single work process (baking cornbread) has two active threads. Then, when you fold the wet into the dry, the threads join and only a single thread is active.

In this case, each thread can be seen as a single task. The next item in the workflow (folding all ingredients together)

Multithreading May Be Hazardous to Your Reliability

We know of a shop that occasionally tries to multithread large, urgent projects. This organization has very effective systems in place for tracking single threads from customer order to completion. However, these systems are not designed to handle the coordination of multithreaded projects. So, these projects invariably are highly stressful and disruptive, slowing more normal work.

If there's a good reason to support multithreading in your organization, by all means do so. If, on the other hand, the need for it is rare, you may wish to consider such work outside your range, as it adds considerably to management overhead.

requires the completion of both threads. When a single work process is multithreaded, the threads eventually come together in this way.

Multithreading adds complexity to the management process. Note that it does not in any way reduce the total amount of work: the team still needed to mix the wet ingredients and mix the dry ingredients. In fact, in a more complex project, there would be some coordination overhead that would actually increase the workload, possibly significantly.

Why multithread, then? Multithreading can reduce the duration of the workflow, from beginning to end. Multithreading a project is usually worth the effort only if there's some urgency to

When in Doubt, Try Redundancy

In some high-touch service businesses, like advertising, a customer will respond to a project in one of two ways: either they'll like it or they won't like it. It's impossible to know in advance. But an organization can sometimes improve its chances by involving the customer from the start, by presenting choices. It begins the project with redundancy: it will start two campaigns, planning to go with whichever the customer prefers. In this case, the duplication of effort constitutes two separate threads. Their interaction is not very close, so the additional overhead is small. In fact, the more independent the two efforts, the better. In this case, the organization shortens the duration of the negotiation phase and increases the chances of a "go" decision.

the final delivery. It can also be helpful if your team's total work-load is unsteady. Multithreading can use idle resources at times of low demand and free up resources for possible later peaks.

Large-scale project management is largely about multi-threading. This is a very useful abstraction in planning and it's at the heart of formal project management techniques like PERT and Gantt charts.

Types of Work Processes

As we defined it earlier, a work process refers to any set of one or more tasks that achieves a particular objective. We catego-rize work processes into four types: projects, routines, cycles, and background work.

Projects

For our purposes, a project is any commitment, no matter how small, that has a definite intended moment of completion and a definite set of conditions that are expected to occur by that moment. The main thing that distinguishes a project from other types of work is that it has a moment of completion associated with it.

> **Key Term**
>
> **Project** A commitment of time and resources aimed at a specific outcome. Projects typically have a deadline, a date by which they are to be completed.

The project in this sense is the basic unit of planning, just as the task is the basic unit of execu-tion. You have other sorts of work processes to man-age, but the project is the source and end of the problems. The project is where you make commitments and where you suc-ceed or fail to meet your commitments.

We use the word "project" less grandly than it's used in the formal literature of "project management." The term "project management" usually refers to very large efforts involving many person-years of effort. Managing such undertakings is certainly a very useful skill. (You may have learned this material and be successfully applying it.)

Even project managers responsible for only a single large project at a time can be overwhelmed by a plethora of small commitments and narrow deadlines as well as large and intermediate matters, just like the rest of us. It's that jungle of commitments that we're concerned with here.

To consider a work process a project, we insist that there be a due date associated with it. Work that has no deadline is

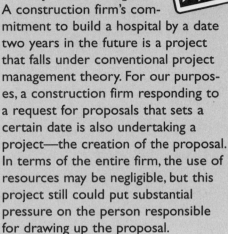

A Project to Propose a Project

A construction firm's commitment to build a hospital by a date two years in the future is a project that falls under conventional project management theory. For our purposes, a construction firm responding to a request for proposals that sets a certain date is also undertaking a project—the creation of the proposal. In terms of the entire firm, the use of resources may be negligible, but this project still could put substantial pressure on the person responsible for drawing up the proposal.

often neglected. So as you manage multiple projects, make sure you have due dates and stick to them.

Routines

Routines, in contrast with projects, are like "a woman's work" in Grandma's day: it's never done. Just as there will always be more laundry to wash, there will always be those weekly staff meetings, those time sheets, that monthly sales spreadsheet, the inbox.

For planning purposes, the routines of importance are the ones that occur daily, weekly, or monthly. Routines that are quarterly or annual tend not to have much impact on your average weekly time allocation. (Relatively rare but repeating events are treated below, under "Cycles.")

Routine A predictable, ongoing demand on your time, for which you don't ever expect completion or finality. A print shop foreman who meets with his pressmen every morning to review work scheduled for that day is practicing a very important routine. All activities that can be routinized should be—considerable stress is avoided as a result of the predictability of routines.

Different people in different circumstances have dramatically different routine workloads. A highly specialized engineer, for example, ideally has a very small load of routine work, while a clerical worker has very little project work. For all those of us falling between the extremes, the amount of project work we can accomplish depends critically on the routines that are also among our responsibilities.

Routines are important. A routine can be like the butterfly that changes the course of a hurricane. Small efforts can have huge consequences.

It's often the case that a routine of five minutes a week can make the difference between success and failure in an operation. For example, neglecting to enter all the billables into the accounting system one week could result in financial problems that ruin a small business.

Don't Abandon Your Routines in a Crisis

The routines of a workgroup are generally not exciting, but they're critical. They should not be sacrificed for high-pressure projects—only for the most extreme emergencies. If you neglect to maintain systems that are set up to sustain an operation, a single success now on a project may lead to multiple failures later.

We're avoiding the word "routine" as an adjective describing a task, as in "Oh, that's just a routine oil change." We reserve the word to refer to demands on your time that recur at predictable intervals, and which, like washing the dishes, may be temporarily completed but never truly go away. Still, it's worth thinking about the value of getting used to things. We'll call this habituation.

There's quite a lot of psychology involved in learning a skill or a job. When you're new to an activity, you think of each separate piece and are very conscious of every small item. (Remember learning to drive, for instance.) Once you've completely learned an activity, it becomes automatized—it's represented very differently in the brain.

When an activity becomes automatized, it falls out of awareness. You hardly even know you're doing it. You're not using

> ### Don't Resist Routines out of Boredom
> A potential client called us in because his workplace was very stressful. His processes were ill-defined and the operation frequently got tangled. We started offering solutions on how to systematize and build routines. He ended up rejecting the solutions. He realized that he had been capable of solving most of the problems himself all along. He actually said, "Yeah, this would work—and I'd be really bored. This is not an intrinsically interesting business. I have to make my work more difficult or I couldn't stand it." (We lost the job.)
>
> Don't make this mistake. Systematize your work, and you'll be able to move your attentions elsewhere. Even if you're adventurous, routines are your friend. Find your adventure elsewhere than in repeating problems and maintaining stress levels.

conscious attention. As a result, the activity becomes much easier and less stressful.

Cycles

In upcoming chapters we'll be advocating for a weekly cycle to get your routines in place. Some workplaces have predictable cycles that are longer than a week, though, and this complicates the picture somewhat.

The classic example of a cyclical workplace is the accountant's office. An accountant has a great deal to achieve every April. The nature of the workflow is very different in March and early April than, say, in October.

Workflow design in an accountancy firm has to take this

> ### The Toy Business: A Seasonal Cycle to the Extreme
> A very large mail order toy manufacturer does extensive brand development and marketing for 11 months out of the year. Then, between Thanksgiving and Christmas, the situation changes dramatically—and predictably—with a burst in demand for clerical labor. During that month, everyone in the company, including the CEO, responds to the peak demand by answering phones, doing clerical work, or packaging and shipping. Then, after the peak phase of the cycle, they return to functioning much as any other corporate office.

cycle into account. The best way to balance the workload is to accomplish as much as possible outside of tax season, knowing full well that little else will be achieved during the months leading up to April 15.

Another example of a cyclical workplace is a magazine publisher. With a bimonthly magazine, for example, work changes according to the two-month cycle. Workplaces like this need to have a planning strategy that takes the cycle into account. The key is balancing the workload. Move as much work as is feasible away from the busy times.

Background Work

Background work is work that is neither routine nor project-driven. It is the sort of work that you do "when you have nothing else to do".

In a perfectly efficient world, it would be possible to schedule 100 per cent of every worker's time, with no overtime and no unproductive time. In the real world, this ideal is not something that can be consistently attained. Nevertheless, salaried workers incur costs for the organization, so it is good to have some secondary tasks for them to fall back on when no immediate duties are pressing.

Self-paced training is an ideal example of a background task. Idled workers can be asked to read relevant training materials and do exercises when there is nothing to do immediately. This sort of activity adds value to the organization, but not as directly as fulfilling time-based commitments.

Background projects need not be low-value, though. Consultants, for example, can use background task time to write a book about their experiences! Lower skilled staff can be asked to "work on straightening out the basement" or "purging the files" at times when there are no pressing requirements.

There is no need to have a plethora of background projects. For most people, having a single background project at a time is ideal. A good background task to have is something that will take a long time to complete, that can be completed in relatively small pieces, that has no urgency, but that will add value when completed.

Meetings

A lot has been written elsewhere about meetings, so we'll just convey the common wisdom. Meetings are often incredibly inefficient because they use up a lot of people's time dealing with trivial matters. However, meetings are absolutely necessary because they keep everyone on the same page, working together. The tradeoff differs dramatically from industry to industry and workgroup to workgroup. Every workgroup needs some internal meetings; but, beyond that basic truism, it's difficult to provide guidance for how many, how frequently, how long.

It's clear that the number of people at a meeting should always be the minimum required to be effective. Involving more people in a meeting not only makes a bigger dent in productivity, but it decreases the chance that any participant is contributing in a meaningful way. All-staff meetings should be very strictly time-limited.

> **Keep Meetings Short**
>
> Smart Managing
>
> The more internal people attending a meeting, the more it costs. Be rigorous with setting agendas and durations for meetings and then adhering to the schedule— and especially when many people are involved.

We bring meetings up here not to offer any unusual advice in this regard, but because they provide some difficulty for our "taskonomy." Internal meetings are not very thread-like, since they occupy more than one staff member at the same time. It's best to treat these as one-off tasks that apply to each person attending the meeting.

Slack

It's not realistic to expect a perfect match between outside demands on your team and the capacity of your team. If the demands exceed the capacity, you will fall further and further

Encourage Play if You Can

An engineering firm had a basketball hoop out in the parking lot. The engineers would frequently play pick-up games, sometimes during business hours. Somebody would take a break and say, "Let's play ball!" Suddenly, 15 engineers would be out there dribbling and shooting, running and jumping.

A partner in the firm tells the story of moving to a new building. In the process of design, the partners explicitly decided to put up a basketball goal at the new location. They recognized that group play contributed to the spirit of the engineering team, with the result that staff members were more likely to put up with occasional long hours and grueling work when such situations arose.

A business that values group play enough to make it acceptable to drop work and play ball is a business where employees will go the extra mile when it is needed.

behind. The only option is to have capacity that exceeds the demand, at least occasionally.

Excess capacity may be expensive, but without excess capacity it's impossible to ensure reliable performance. Therefore, you must expect that some of the time your team members will have fulfilled all of their project and routine responsibilities.

There are two ways to handle this excess capacity—the formal and the informal. We recommend a healthy mix of the two.

Formal slack is directed at non-critical development. The main possibilities are to develop skills or to develop the business. Team members can read work-related materials, get formal training, do broad research, redesign company fliers and internal documents, or even improve the work Web site. This sort of development is especially important for managers, and we'll have more to say about it in Chapter 8.

Informal slack is pure play. Basically, you tolerate any activity that is not actively disruptive to the business. This can be an effective morale builder, especially if different team members encounter slack at the same time. Some organizations that depend on creativity actually cultivate ways to make the most of slack time.

Manager's Checklist for Chapter 4

❑ To begin formal planning, a manager must understand the various types of work and how they relate to one another—what we call "taskonomy."

❑ Tasks are the fundamental atomic unit of work. A task is work that a single person can accomplish in a single day without interruption.

❑ Boundaries between tasks can cause trouble. Handoffs should be considered as part of the task.

❑ Workload is the total number of work hours put in by the team on a work process. Duration is the time between the group's acceptance of a work process and its completion.

❑ Most work consists of a number of tasks. Usually these tasks are organized into one or more sequences, called threads.

❑ A work process with more than one active thread is called multithreaded. Multithreading is not always possible and not always desirable. Multithreading reduces duration but usually adds to workload.

❑ A routine is work that occurs on a regular basis and that is not expected to end. It's best scheduled to a particular part of the week and assigned to particular person or group. Habituation to a task may cause some boredom, but it also reduces stress, releasing energy for other efforts.

❑ A cycle is the pattern of a workload that changes with the month or the seasons. Cyclic work presents special planning problems.

❑ It's impossible to reach 100% efficiency in assignments without falling behind or allowing quality to suffer. During slack times, staff should have activities to keep occupied productively.

❑ A certain amount of pure play in the workplace can be very healthy for morale.

What's on
Your Plate?

We're moving toward managing the workload of an entire team to effectively complete projects. We'll begin in this chapter with the simpler exercise of examining your own personal workload as a manager.

There are two reasons to start with your own workload as a preliminary exercise. The first reason is familiarity. This is the part of the situation with which you are most familiar—you know what you're doing, presumably, better than you know what any staff member is doing! The second reason is that, as a manager, you set the tone for the group. Few staff will feel inclined to show growth in any area beyond the level you yourself attain. If you personally seem to be perpetually in crisis, the members of your group won't take seriously your efforts to move your group toward more reliable performance. So let's take a close look at how you parcel out your own time.

Are You Overloaded and Overwhelmed?

If you're reading this book, if you need to improve your skills in managing multiple projects, you probably fall behind occasionally. Perhaps you took over a job that was vacant for a while or you took over part of someone else's responsibilities when that individual could not cope with all of them. Perhaps there was some unexpected circumstance that caused you to fall behind.

Often, as consultants, we find that our customers describe themselves as "overwhelmed." They feel overloaded. One of our first tasks is to help them decide objectively how overloaded they are. In this chapter we'll help you apply our method to your situation.

There are two parts to being overwhelmed. The first is the sheer *complexity* of the tasks that we find ourselves facing. The second is an *emotional* component.

Falling behind engenders feelings of confusion and frustration. To make matters worse, such confusion and frustration are stresses that impair performance, which then adds to the overload. It's a vicious circle.

The vicious circle is a bad situation for anyone, but it has special ramifications for people in positions of responsibility. As a manager, your anxiety and uncertainty rub off on your team. A confused and anxious leader makes for a confused and anxious team. The fact that others are taking their marching orders from you means that your stress is amplified and propagated through the whole team. The cycle of stress and chaos now infects everyone.

"Too Busy to Get Organized"

The most common example of an overload/performance vicious circle is the messy desk.

Suppose that you're already very busy and someone wants a document urgently. The document does not turn up where you expect it, so you go rifling through every stack of papers in sight, moving your best-laid plans for document management closer to a tossed salad. Now suppose (hooray!) that you find the document. What do you do? Do you recover from the mess you've just made? No, because you're "too busy." Is this saving time? In the short run, yes, because it would take at least a few minutes to just put things back in order. But in the long run, you're likely to have even more trouble the next time you need a document. That's not a wise tradeoff.

Consider the manager who is uncertain how to proceed, frustrated, and quick to anger. When a staff is uncertain and demoralized as a result of the manager's frustration, one result is an unhealthy feedback loop that increasingly hurts productivity. Members of that manager's staff may be diligently pursuing a path that the manager believes has already changed or may be at loose ends with nothing to do. Because the manager is frustrated and short-tempered, the staff may be unwilling to close the loop, uncertain whether the boss's frustration will erupt as disapproval.

It's your first responsibility as an overloaded manager in a situation where you're managing multiple projects to get out from under. If you're in a situation of exhaustion, confusion, and burnout, it's essential to pull out of it before putting new systems in place. This chapter and the next will help you do so. Then, the rest of the book will help you set up systems to attain a sustainable and efficient operation.

The Warning Signs

How do you know when you've bitten off more than you can chew? There are a number of classic warning signs of overload:

Some Crunch Can Be Healthy

As Tom DeMarco points out in his wonderful recent management book *Slack: Getting Past Burnout, Busywork, and the Myth of Total Efficiency* (New York: Broadway Books, 2001), the occasional crunch period can be a good thing. If you deal with it effectively, it can be motivating—it can extract that little bit extra from you and your team. What's more, a successful delivery under pressure can be good for morale and team building.

Look for the middle ground. If you never find yourself in a crunch, you may be missing out on opportunities for growth. This experience can be misleading, though, because a team in a perpetual crunch environment is typically less effective than a team that works reasonable hours. The increases in effectiveness and morale are unsustainable and reverse quickly.

- Lots of overtime
- Lots of wasted time
- People doing other people's jobs
- Consistently late deliveries
- Consistently disappointing quality
- Constantly shifting priorities
- Some people working much harder than others, causing mutual resentment
- Poor morale

The overloaded team often is producing results, and income, at a substantial rate. The overloaded team may even be quite profitable, discouraging the systematic change that will eventually be required to retain customers. However, much of the team's efforts are being wasted on friction and inefficiency— and the risk of turnover of key personnel is very high.

Often in such situations, you could be achieving as much or more, doing it better, and having more fun. That's what this book is about!

The problem is getting from here to there. It's very important to understand that if you're overwhelmed, you can't improve your processes! Getting your team from stressed to smoothly functioning requires thought and planning on your part, and effort and patience on the part of all concerned. The paradox of workplace change is that the time when you most need the change is exactly the time when you are least able to afford the resources to achieve it.

Don't Fix Your Systems When You're Overloaded

The temptation, and even the pressure, to immediately find a better way to do things can be very high when you're swamped. That's the wrong time to fix your systems, though. You need to get things under control first. Then you and your team can find the time and energy to troubleshoot and improve your methods.

In other words, when you're swamped you need to bail out and paddle for shore. You'll be in a better position to patch your boat once you're high and dry.

So the first step is to cut yourself some slack. No, we're not recommending laziness. Rather, we're recommending that you somehow carve out the time and energy that you'll need to achieve your objectives of building a happy and productive work environment.

How Much Time Do You Have to Work With?

The following time management exercise is one we've developed and used successfully with many of our clients, both individuals and groups. It's easier to understand how it applies to an individual, though, so we'll start by getting you, personally, out from under.

The first step is to take an inventory of what you have to do. One of the main points we'll be making in this book is that it pays to have a good bird's-eye view of what you're doing. (Throughout the rest of the chapter, we're assuming that you or your team is in a time crunch. If you aren't, skim this chapter for now and then remember to keep it in reserve for a rainy day.)

Before you begin inventorying your responsibilities, decide if you're a two-key-ring person or a single-key-ring person. (This idea isn't original to us. We'd like to credit the originator, but Michael read about it a very long time ago. We'd appreciate hearing from anyone who can identify the origin of the observation.) There are two main strategies for dealing with work. One is the integrated strategy, where work is mingled with personal life and it's hardly clear where one ends and the other begins. People who live in that way tend to have all their keys on one key ring. The other is the differentiated strategy, where work time and personal time are sharply distinguished. Such people often have two separate key rings, one for home and one for work.

The exercise is more complicated if you're a one-key-ring person. In that case, when we take inventory of your responsibilities, we have to account for every aspect of your life (cooking, friends, fitness, visits to the in-laws, soccer coaching...). Still, you know exactly how many hours there are in a day (24) and days in a week (7).

The Key Ring Concept

How you keep track of your keys can provide insights into how you organize your life.

Is your personal life sharply distinct from your work life? Do you have a rich family life that you keep very separate from the stresses of the workplace? We'll call you a two-key-ring person. You need to be very specific about how much of your time you're realistically going to devote to the workplace.

Are you constantly moving back and forth from work to home in your thoughts and your activities? Is your work an expression of your personality? Are there times when you aren't sure if you're at work or play? Then you're a one-key-ring person. You need to include all of your activities in your time inventory.

On the other hand, if you're a two-key-ring person, you save yourself a lot of complexity. There are fewer items to account for in your time inventory. But you have to make one very difficult determination. How much time do you have available to deal with your work?

Let's presume that the remainder of the book succeeds in keeping you out of perpetual crisis. We won't promise that you'll never see a crunch, but we'll guarantee that you'll spend most of your time safely outside of this frantic level of work commitment. So assume that the current situation is temporary.

Decide, realistically, how much time you have available for work and commuting to work. State this as a number of hours per week. Also be clear as to how many days a week this represents. (For most two-key-ring people the workweek has five days.) The number you are looking for is the maximum weekly work time that you could sustain for a few months if you could be confident that it would get lighter after that. Promise yourself a week off when things lighten up.

Your Availability

We'll call your maximum weekly work hours your availability. This is the raw material out of which you must build a realistic plan.

It's important to understand where your time is going. Often, people neglect significant time sinks when they plan. For example, we know a person who moved into a house that was 30 miles from his place of employment. Although these were almost all highway miles, he commuted during rush hour, so he was spending well over an hour each way. It took him several months before he allowed himself to realize that he was spending close to 15 hours a week commuting

> **Smart Managing**
>
> ## Estimate Availability Realistically
>
> If you're dealing with a work crunch, planning your way through it begins with a realistic estimate of how many hours per week a work maximum could be. Be honest with yourself about where your time is going.

When you estimate weekly availability, use the maximum number of hours you could work and still gain net productivity.

There's a subtle point here. An hour in which you can work productively isn't necessarily an hour that's worth working, even if you have no concerns other than work! There is some number of hours beyond which every hour you work actually decreases your total productivity!

You don't believe it? Draw a crude graph of productivity per week versus hours worked per week. Label the hours axis from zero to 168 (the total hours in a week, 24 x 7).

As you add hours, your total production increases more or less steadily, until you start getting tired and making mistakes. Then the slope of the line becomes less steep and you accomplish less for each additional hour, though your total production continues to increase (see Figure 5-1). Eventually, the curve has to turn around altogether, though, because the productivity at 168 hours per week is exactly zero (see Figure 5-2).

If you were really to try to work every hour in a week without any rest at all, you would quickly become very sick and your productivity would be no different than if you had worked no hours at all! In addition, you would enjoy this down time much less than you would a vacation.

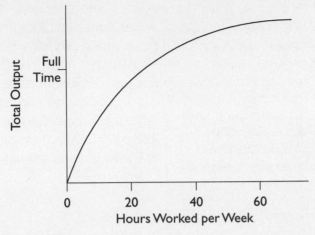

Figure 5-1. Ouput increases with effort, with diminishing returns

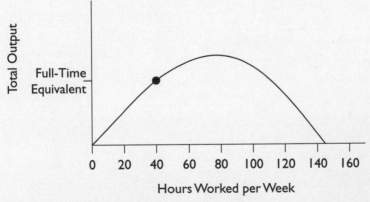

Figure 5-2. After too many hours, output drops off, not only per hour, but in total. In this example, working beyond 80 hours is pointless

Where the curve turns around differs from person to person and job to job. Also, people can sustain a huge effort for a week or two that they can't sustain for months. In any case, the overall shape of the curve is inescapable.

When you imagine working 168 hours a week, this effect is obvious, but in practice it can be subtle. If your turning point is at 70 hours, you've added very little work between the 60th and

Avoid Habitual Heroics
Putting in too many hours in a crisis reduces productivity, not simply per hour but actually in total. It's hard to see this turning point. Returns can begin diminishing at not much over a standard workweek, making further efforts counterproductive. An occasional extraordinary effort can save the day, but demanding such effort every day is futile.

70th hours. You should not have bothered. You'll accomplish some work in your 71st hour. The problem is that it will make you sufficiently tired and stressed somewhere in the other 70 hours that you'll have a net loss of work anyway!

Your Project Portfolio

We often find that the overly informal workplace lacks a clear listing of in-process project work. In those cases, our work begins by identifying those projects. We call a complete listing of the projects for a workgroup the *project portfolio*.

Project portfolio The set of all current deadline-driven commitments that a group or individual is currently working on. Having a clear list of active commitments is the first step in evaluating whether they can all be met.

Among the simplest pieces of advice we frequently offer is to have a complete project portfolio—in other words, a clear list of active commitments. This is in essence a big-picture view of your responsibilities—an important step in managing multiple projects.

Add up Your Projects

For the present exercise, we're looking for your personal list of commitments. If you haven't maintained such a list in the past, this is a good time to begin. (Also, if you haven't maintained a personal list of commitments, you ought to do some studying in the ample literature of personal time management.)

Identify Your Immediate Projects

Because we're dealing with a crunch that we hope is finite, we limit this exercise to projects that are due fairly soon. Focus on the most distant deadline that you're presently worrying about and deadlines before that date.

However, you can't neglect work on projects due after the crunch! We'll talk about factoring them back in after we complete the exercise.

Time Management System

Whether with a paper organizer or an electronic one, almost every successful professional has mastered the four basic functions of personal organizing:

• the personal calendar
• the to-do list
• the address book
• the memo pad

If you don't have such a system now, it would be a good idea to get one and to learn the basics of time management. See Appendix for suggested readings.

Now, make a list of those short-run projects. If possible, list them out loud to a sympathetic person. (You have special dispensation to whine. This rare privilege will encourage you to complain about everything you have to do, which on any other occasion would be rude!) Make your list complete.

You should end up with a list of every deadline and every vague promise that you've made that someone expects you to keep in the next six months. (If you're a one-key-ring person, this includes obligations to friends and family!)

Estimate the Hours for Each Project

The next step is to estimate the total number of hours you think it will take of your personal time to complete the project. (One-key-ring people: include commitments in every area of your life. Two-key-ring people: you may be able to get away with estimating only work commitments. You may decide based on how overwhelmed you feel.) Depending on the project and your level of experience, this can be a more or less difficult task. Let's not

Don't Double Count

If a project has milestones, don't count the hours toward each milestone and toward completion. For instance, if you're making a cake and it takes a half hour to mix the ingredients and an hour to bake it, count that as an hour and a half of commitment, not a half hour to mix the ingredients and 90 minutes to make the cake, for a total of two hours! Yes, it seems silly when it's something as simple as a cake, but keep your eye on the principle. Time expended toward a milestone or a sub-project shouldn't be counted again in figuring the load of the larger project.

hear anything about "garbage in, garbage out," though. You're quite capable of estimating how your skills apply to your commitments or you would never have taken on those commitments. We're not looking for perfection here, just your best bet.

For example, you can imagine yourself musing, "Hmm, writing that article for the *Moose Jaw Gazette* on Pokemon mania in Alberta, well, I'll have to do some research, say about 12 hours, and six hours to write the thing, another two hours after I get the editorial markups, hmm, about 20 hours." Or "sponge painting the reception room, well, painting the living room takes about five hours a coat, and that room is about the same size, and I have no idea about the sponge part, but I guess that's like an extra coat, so, hmmm, 15 hours." Notice that you may have to break some projects down into steps to help you make the estimate.

Write down the estimated total number of hours next to each project. Do not include any time other than your own concentrated effort. Do not count time when the progress of the project is in the hands of a subordinate, vendor, customer, or your uncle's second cousin. Do, however, count any one-off items (correspondence, travel, etc.) that may be lurking in your to-do list or on your calendar.

You begin to see where we're going with this, don't you? We're going to decide whether it's possible for you to do everything you're committed to.

Get the Due Date for Each Project

You'll also need a due date for each project. Sometimes there's a formal deadline and sometimes the commitment is vague. This is how vague commitments get lost in the shuffle. Set yourself a deadline for each vague commitment.

Your Background Routines

Now we've established how many hours you have to work with, what projects you need to accomplish in those hours, and how long each will take. Are we in a position to determine whether your load is in the realm of possibility yet?

Not yet. We're missing an important piece of the puzzle—your routines.

Here again, you should make a complete list. So complain to your accomplice. List everything you're expected to do on a regular basis. Identify every routine that you regularly perform to sustain your operation. Identify time-consuming activities from which you wish you could escape but can't.

Then estimate how many hours per week you need to put into such routines. (For daily routines, multiply by the number of days in your week—usually five for two-key-ring folks, six or seven for one-key-ring people.)

Since we're presuming you're in a crunch, take a minimum amount of time for these items and plan to delegate as much of this work as possible.

If you're taking the single-key-ring whole-life inventory approach, this category will be very large, as it includes such hard-to-delegate items as eating and sleeping. For a two-key-ring work-only time inventory, the proportion of routine can vary practically from 0% to 100%.

Tasks, Interruptions, Distractions, and Overhead

Before we go adding it all up, be careful to consider all the items that take up your time that aren't formal responsibilities. For many people, the biggest one of these is commuting.

Answering phone calls and e-mails, dealing with small tasks as they come up, unexpected meetings with subordinates or supervisors on various problems—all these also place demands on your time. Perhaps you read trade magazines or search the Internet on a regular basis. Realistically assess how much time you're putting into various activities before closing out your list of routines.

Spreadsheet Program

Most people these days use Microsoft Excel™ for the sort of calculation described here, but there are many alternatives, including Star Office™, available for free downloading at http://www.sun.com/star/staroffice/.

In any case, a manager without a spreadsheet program is like a taxi driver without a steering wheel. Get one!

Crunch Time

OK, now it's time to complete the inventory.

Pull out a calendar and create a blank spreadsheet (or, if you must, get some grid paper). We'll describe the process as if it were done with a pencil on a paper grid. If you have basic spreadsheet skills, you should be able to fill in the blanks as needed.

Step 1: Chart Your Time Line

In the first column of the first row, put the word "Item." In the following columns of that row, put the date of each Monday from the beginning of the period.

In the example in Figure 5-3, we're tracking the first six weeks of a year.

Step 2: Chart Your Availability

In the next row (you may leave a row blank for easier reading), put in each column an estimate of the total number of hours you will be available in that week.

In the example, you're generally available 50 hours per week. One week you're less available due to travel. In the most critical week, you imagine you can squeeze out an extra 10 hours of work.

ITEM	2 Jan	9 Jan	16 Jan	23 Jan	30 Jan	6 Feb
Availability	50	50	32	50	60	20 Feb
Routine						
reports	3	3	3	3	6	3
meetings	4	6		4	4	4
calls	2	2		2	2	2
Project						
Bubbles			10			10
Blossom	8	8	8	72		
Buttercup					120	
Total	17	19	21	81	132	19
Cumulative Total Commitments	17	36	57	138	270	289
Cumulative Availability	50	100	132	182	242	292
Surplus	33	64	75	44	-28	3

Figure 5-3. A spreadsheet analysis of crunch time

Step 3: Chart Your Commitments

In the leftmost column, list all routines and all projects that will have a significant impact on your time budget over the period you're tracking.

In the example, you've identified three routines and three projects that you expect to take up significant time in the first six weeks of the year.

In real life, your calculations will probably show many more items than these. This example is intended to be complicated enough to show how the method works, but no more.

Step 4: Estimate the Time to Completion for Each Project

Even leaving aside the difficulty of making estimates, this part is a little tricky. If no deliverable is due until the last week of a project, so that you can allocate your time freely over the period, put the entire estimate in the week that the delivery is due. If partial deliveries are due, put the total corresponding to the partial delivery in the intervening weeks and the remainder in the week that the whole project is to be delivered.

In our example, you escape some of your routines in the third week when you're traveling, but otherwise you need to put time into these routines weekly. You need to budget extra time at the end of the month for monthly reports, as well, and there's an extra corporate meeting scheduled for two hours in the second week.

Project Buttercup has no intermediate deliveries, but you estimate you need to put 120 hours into it over the five weeks before it is due, so you put the figure 120 in the fifth week. Project Blossom is deliverable in the fourth week and will take about 96 hours, of which at least eight you need to deliver in each of the intervening weeks. Finally, project Bubbles has deliverables in the third and sixth weeks and you anticipate 10 hours' work for each of them.

Step 5: Get the Weekly Total of Your Commitments

In the first column of a new row, write *Weekly Total*. Then, in each subsequent column, total the numbers in that column (not counting your availability). This number is not very useful—it indicates how many hours of work come due in that particular week.

Please note that you should only add up hours in the week that they are due. Later in the exercise, we'll distribute the work over the weeks prior to their due date. If there are no intermediate deliveries, the entire time estimate will go in the column of the week the work is due.

Step 6: Get the Cumulative Total of Your Commitments

The more useful number is the cumulative total. This indicates how much work you'll need to do in total before the end of each week to fulfill all responsibilities due by then. This number is the total of all totals to date. Create a row under *Weekly Total* and name it *Cumulative Total Commitments*. In the first column, the cumulative total is the same as the total for the week. In each subsequent column, the cumulative total is that week's total plus the previous week's cumulative total. For example, 21 hours of work are due in the third week; the previous week's cumulative total was 36 hours, so the cumulative total for the third week is $36 + 21 = 57$.

Step 7: Get Your Cumulative Availability

Create a new row and label it *Cumulative Availability*. Accumulate your availability as you accumulated your commitment. That is, the first week's cumulative availability is the same as the first week's availability (50 hours). Each subsequent week's cumulative availability is the week's availability plus the previous week's cumulative availability.

This number is the total number of hours you're available to work up through the given weeks.

Step 8: Compute Your Time Surplus

In each column, subtract your cumulative commitment from your cumulative availability. This result should be positive for each column. This number tells you how many hours of slack you have to complete all the assignments due up through that week.

> **Critical date (crunch date)** The critical date, informally known as crunch date, is the date for which your time resources are maximally committed. That's the date that's critical to your planning. In the exercise this is the date with your largest time deficit or smallest time surplus (if there is no deficit).

In our example, in column 5, we have a deficit rather than a surplus. The fifth week is the critical date. This is the week in which we will have the greatest difficulty meeting commitments.

In this case, we have committed 28 hours more than we have available over the five-week period. We need an average of almost six hours per week more than our original estimated availability or we need to trim the number of hours from some of the tasks (perhaps by delegation, perhaps by increased efficiency) or we need to accept that something will be late and we can begin to plan what that will be.

About Time Deficits

It's important to understand that the purpose of the calculation is to identify the crunch week and determine the time surplus or deficit for that week. The surplus or deficit for any previous week does not take into account the items due in the critical date and isn't meaningful.

In the example, 270 hours of work must be completed in the first five weeks and only 242 hours are available. The fact that 50 hours are available in the first week to complete only 17 hours of deliverables is not important. Those extra 33 hours and then some must be committed to later deliveries. The fact that 292 hours are available in the first six weeks to do 289 hours of work should offer no solace, as 270 of them must be done in the first five weeks.

If you find the calculations a bit confusing, please note the following—only the smallest surplus or largest deficit is meaningful in this calculation.

In practice, we usually find that, unless there has been an unexpected change in conditions, most people make commitments that are just barely possible.

Notice that there are no contingencies built into our estimates. Depending on how uncertain the estimates are and how firm the deadlines are, it may pay to make time estimates that are conservative, that is, on the high side. Even so, the best-laid plans of mice and men often go astray.

The best situation, then, is that your crunch week (the week with the smallest time surplus) still has an ample surplus.

If you have a deficit, but it's not too big, perhaps you can find some way to catch up—maybe move the monthly report out a couple of weeks or so. Still, plan to work very hard until the crunch date.

We've done this exercise with our clients dozens of times, and we've noticed an interesting pattern. Almost every time, even if the client has done no formal planning at all, the result is that the work is barely possible if everything goes right. People have a good idea of their capacities, but a weak ability to account for bad breaks or unexpected setbacks.

Most often, we find that people who don't plan are a little too close to the edge, but not quite over it.

If you are overloaded or are living too close to the edge habitually, keep reading. In the next chapter we'll offer up some ideas as to what to do about it.

Manager's Checklist for Chapter 5

❑ Overload and performance problems can form a vicious circle. It's a good idea to break the loop as early as possible.

❑ Managers who allow themselves to become overloaded and overwhelmed can have a direct negative impact on the performance of their team.

❑ Heroic efforts cannot be sustained and quickly become counterproductive.

❑ The extent of overload can be quantified and can form the basis for a formal plan.

❑ It's a good idea to have an exhaustive list of your current projects easily accessible at all times and to keep aware of them. In fact, it's a bad idea not to do so.

❑ Although estimates are always uncertain, workload estimates are the essence of workflow planning. A crude estimate is much better than no estimate at all.

❑ You should list all of your commitments before a critical date, add up time estimates for each of them, and decide if you'll be able to meet them all.

Out from Under

If you completed the exercise in the last chapter, you ended up with a critical date (the date that determines how busy you need to be) and a number of hours per week that you need to put in above or below what you have available.

In the chapters that follow, we'll discuss how to extend that method to your entire group so you can actually meet your project commitments.

How Busy Are You?

There are three possible outcomes of the exercise: you don't have enough time, you have barely enough time if everything goes well, or you have ample time.

If you aren't able to fulfill your commitments, this chapter is for you. We'll discuss how to extract yourself from a crisis. Most of our advice in this chapter will be simple common sense. At stressful times, though, simple common sense can be very useful!

If you're barely able to fulfill your commitments, don't let your guard down. Note that all your estimates were just that—it's not always easy to predict how long a particular endeavor will take or what unexpected concerns may arise.

Day: thurs Date: 3/25

Time: 4 PM Service: S/color

Designer: Kim

To receive your prebook discount please keep the appointment.

HAIR EXCITEMENT

KINGS HIGHWAY PLAZA
STRATHAM, NH

(603) 772-9600

WALK-INS WELCOME   APPOINTMENTS APPRECIATED

SUNDAY 10:00 - 5:00
MONDAY 12:00 - 9:00
TUES - FRI 9:00 - 9:00
SATURDAY 9:00 - 5:00

If you're easily able to fulfill your commitments, don't skip too lightly through this chapter, since the material here will be extended to your whole team later on. What's

Overcommitted?
If you think you may be overcommitted, please don't read this chapter until you've completed the exercise described in Chapter 5.

more, even if your current workload is realistic, you may wish to use these methods to help a staff member that you supervise get caught up.

So, although this chapter is intended to help you deal with overload, read on even if your time is currently under control.

Overload

So you're overloaded! You suspected as much, didn't you?

At this point, you may feel worse than when you started. Clear evidence of overcommitment can be daunting. Consider, though, that you've made

Work with Your Ally
In the last chapter, we advised you to get a "sympathetic person" to help you inventory your workload. If you're overloaded, don't let go of this ally. Ask him or her to help you, not by doing your work, but by helping you to plan your way out of the crunch.

If your ally is a consultant, of course you'll need to pay that person. The alternative is to draw upon a peer. You can offer to return the favor at a later date.

It's probably not a good idea to draw upon a supervisor or a subordinate in this matter, unless there's no realistic alternative.

real progress in addressing your problem.

The exercise in Chapter 5 has shown you exactly how overloaded you are. Your immediate objective is to get this overload under control. You can't realistically expect to improve your own situation—or that of your workgroup—until you gain control over your current commitments. You now have a number (your deficit in hours) to work on.

Be very careful about just committing yourself to work those extra hours. While each person's capacity for work is different, no one's capacity is unlimited. As we discussed in Chapter 5,

working so many hours that you suffer from exhaustion
undermine your performance. The extra hours may be
than wasted: they may tire you out so much that they r
your total productivity!

One problem is that the deficit that you've identified
greatly discourage you. Addressing this discouragement
important part of coping with overload; indeed, it's often
of the problem.

Why We Get Overloaded

As individuals, we like to be challenged. When we don't
enough to do, we become bored and listless. We like to t
enough work to keep engaged. The closer we get to our
and the more we take advantage of opportunities, the gr
the excitement and the greater the rewards.

In the workplace, these personal motivations are inte
by the needs of our employer to obtain maximum value
the investment in our salary and benefits. The harder we
and the more work we take on, the more exciting and pr
our work is—up to a point.

Consider a highway. We get maximum return on the
ment of our tax dollars when a highway carries as much
as possible, as many vehicles per hour as is safe. In that
the cost per vehicle mile is minimized. We get closer to t
ideal for a given highway with every vehicle on it, until s
there's just a little too much traffic. The vehicles begin to
dramatically more slowly as traffic abruptly exceeds the
ty of the highway. Brake lights come on, snarls develop,
waste time. Not only are individual drivers inconvenienc
the highway is suddenly delivering much less traffic per
than when demand was slightly less.

People, in this way, are much like highways. They do
and more as more and more is demanded of them, reac
state of peak performance. Then, when demands pass a
optimum, performance abruptly plummets. It's importan
understand that the difference in load between peak perf

If you're easily able to fulfill your commitments, don't skip too lightly through this chapter, since the material here will be extended to your whole team later on. What's more, even if your current workload is realistic, you may wish to use these methods to help a staff member that you supervise get caught up.

> **Overcommitted?** ⚠️ CAUTION!
> If you think you may be overcommitted, please don't read this chapter until you've completed the exercise described in Chapter 5.

So, although this chapter is intended to help you deal with overload, read on even if your time is currently under control.

Overload

So you're overloaded! You suspected as much, didn't you?

At this point, you may feel worse than when you started. Clear evidence of overcommitment can be daunting. Consider, though, that you've made real progress in addressing your problem.

> **Work with Your Ally** TRICKS OF THE TRADE
> In the last chapter, we advised you to get a "sympathetic person" to help you inventory your workload. If you're overloaded, don't let go of this ally. Ask him or her to help you, not by doing your work, but by helping you to plan your way out of the crunch.
>
> If your ally is a consultant, of course you'll need to pay that person. The alternative is to draw upon a peer. You can offer to return the favor at a later date.
>
> It's probably not a good idea to draw upon a supervisor or a subordinate in this matter, unless there's no realistic alternative.

The exercise in Chapter 5 has shown you exactly how overloaded you are. Your immediate objective is to get this overload under control. You can't realistically expect to improve your own situation—or that of your workgroup—until you gain control over your current commitments. You now have a number (your deficit in hours) to work on.

Be very careful about just committing yourself to work those extra hours. While each person's capacity for work is different, no one's capacity is unlimited. As we discussed in Chapter 5, working so many hours that you suffer from exhaustion can undermine your performance. The extra hours may be worse than wasted: they may tire you out so much that they reduce your total productivity!

One problem is that the deficit that you've identified can greatly discourage you. Addressing this discouragement is an important part of coping with overload; indeed, it's often a part of the problem.

Why We Get Overloaded

As individuals, we like to be challenged. When we don't have enough to do, we become bored and listless. We like to take on enough work to keep engaged. The closer we get to our limits and the more we take advantage of opportunities, the greater the excitement and the greater the rewards.

In the workplace, these personal motivations are intensified by the needs of our employer to obtain maximum value from the investment in our salary and benefits. The harder we work and the more work we take on, the more exciting and profitable our work is—up to a point.

Consider a highway. We get maximum return on the investment of our tax dollars when a highway carries as much traffic as possible, as many vehicles per hour as is safe. In that case, the cost per vehicle mile is minimized. We get closer to this ideal for a given highway with every vehicle on it, until suddenly there's just a little too much traffic. The vehicles begin to move dramatically more slowly as traffic abruptly exceeds the capacity of the highway. Brake lights come on, snarls develop, people waste time. Not only are individual drivers inconvenienced, but the highway is suddenly delivering much less traffic per hour than when demand was slightly less.

People, in this way, are much like highways. They do more and more as more and more is demanded of them, reaching a state of peak performance. Then, when demands pass a certain optimum, performance abruptly plummets. It's important to understand that the difference in load between peak performance and abrupt collapse can be very slight. It's when things are at their best that the risk of taking on too much is greatest.

This situation keeps happening because there are great pay-offs to maximum productivity. It's fun and profitable. Everyone wants to reach the point where they are making the most of themselves and every organization wants to make the most of its employees.

There are two problems with this ambition. First, most people and many organizations don't have a clear view of their commitment load. The natural tendency is to accept any additional opportunities or responsibilities that arise. Second, life is capricious. Sometimes unexpected obligations or inconveniences arise. These can abruptly push people or groups over the edge, beyond their capacity.

In the long run, good views and careful planning can avoid overloads that result from taking on too many commitments. Overloads due to unexpected events can be reduced by risk management strategies, although they can never be totally eliminated. The best approach, therefore, is to aim your commitments to total slightly below your maximum capacity, to resist the natural inclination to risk one more project.

> ### Seeking the Ideal
> **Smart Managing**
>
> The difference in load between peak performance and total collapse can be very slight. Your ideal load is slightly below your maximum capacity. This gives you the flexibility to accommodate unanticipated projects or commitments that arise.

Overload as a Vicious Circle

Highways get stuck in overload when the demands are too high, because vehicles slow down when the distance between them gets too short. It takes a long time for the highway to clear, since the traffic is moving so slowly. The traffic will continue to move slowly until the highway is clear again! So even if the demand drops to levels below the capacity of the highway, it may not recover for some time.

Computers get stuck in overload when demand on their memory becomes excessive. Even if you release the memory, they may have difficulty recovering from the overload. People are the same way. When a person is overcommitted, there are several reasons that he or she will stay overloaded. One is "thrashing." Like an overloaded computer, an overloaded worker may need to spend a lot of effort just not falling behind. You may find yourself in the situation described by the Red Queen in *Through the Looking Glass:* "It takes all the running you can do to stay in the same place."

Another cause for getting stuck in overload is simple fatigue. You may have been working so hard that you're now too tired to catch up.

Often, the overloaded person has an obvious tactic to get caught up, but simply can't find the time to put the plan in place. A common example is that there are funds for an assistant in the budget, but it may be impossible to pull together the time for hiring or training.

The biggest factor in getting stuck in overload, however, is the emotional component. It's probably not news to you that

---

Key Term

Thrash To move wildly or violently, without accomplishing anything useful. This is a term used to describe the situation when personal computers suffer abrupt drops in performance due to overload, usually because too many programs are running at once. When the demands of the programs exceed the capacity of random access memory (RAM), the system must move data back and forth between RAM and the hard drive. The result is that the disk drive whirls a lot (thrashes), but the computer makes very little progress because it's spending so much time switching among tasks.

Similarly, people with too many projects may spend most of their time just keeping the projects alive without making substantial progress. Their thrashing is a symptom of overload, and it dramatically reduces overall productivity.

If your computer starts thrashing, close a large program. (This may take some time; the computer, after all, is in a very inefficient mode!) If you find yourself thrashing, lighten your load.

> ### Too Busy to Get Help
>
> We're currently consulting with an organization that has a full-time computer and database administrator who's constantly falling behind.
>
> A less experienced assistant was hired to lighten the system administrator's load. The assistant has been on payroll for some months now and complains of not having enough to do—even though the administrator is still desperately behind!
>
> The problem is that the administrator, in addition to having no supervisory or training experience, almost always feels "too busy" to devote time to the assistant. The administrator is stuck in overload, even though help is available!

negative emotions can have a devastating effect on performance. The condition of overload is nothing if not stressful.

Often it's on the emotional side that you need to begin your recovery.

The Emotional Demands of Overload

Emotional stress is a prime symptom and a prime cause of overload.

If you've just completed the exercise of proving to yourself that you're overloaded, you'll probably be feeling especially discouraged. That's why the first step in recovering from overload is to calm down.

You shouldn't be unrealistically cheerful about your predicament. After all, you're in a difficult period. On the other hand, you're trying to get control of your problems, so you should feel better. You won't necessarily come out of the overload situation unscathed, but you can, with care, make the best of the situation and, to do so, you should focus on the positive and not beat yourself up.

So let's look at the up side.

You Are Not Guilty

Shame is an emotion that comes easily to the person who's overcommitted. You may be seen as performing below your proven capacity, and unable to rise to the occasion of unusual demands. You may find yourself just as convinced as others around you that you're selfishly procrastinating exactly when you can least afford it, or that you're wantonly disorganized and unreliable, even untrustworthy.

It's essential that you understand where these feelings come from, whether from within yourself or from a team member or another person you need to work with (or, for that matter, live with). A person who's fallen behind needs courage and encouragement, not shaming, to fully recover. Shame can elicit very simple behaviors (it's important, for example, in toilet training a baby), but it can't be used to elicit highly functional professional performance, because effective performance is essentially impossible in the presence of negative emotions. The natural tendency to express shame when others disappoint you or to feel shame when you disappoint others needs to be minimized.

Your first step, then, is to forgive yourself. Understand that it was with good intentions that you entered the current predicament. Understand that your disappointment with yourself is getting in the way of your recovery. Let go of your stress. A good place to start may even be to take a half-day's vacation!

Notice also that like shame, even pride can get in the way. Pride leads to hubris, which can lead to sloppy performance and alienation of important work associates. Pride can

Ice Cream Therapy

TRICKS OF THE TRADE Take the afternoon off.

Don't make a habit of this, but once in a while if the stress becomes too much for you, take a breather. Walk in the park. Have an ice cream cone.

Consider it an investment: it makes sense to take a half-day of vacation now rather than a whole sick day later in the week. You may need to take this as vacation time rather than sick leave, but take it before your job starts to damage your health.

Often a few hours of playing hooky can do wonders to revitalize an overworked person, increasing his or her output in the end. Of course, this works only in very small doses. Try not to do it too regularly!

Don't Indulge Your Emotions

While we very much encourage you to get an ally to help you ponder these issues, there's a pitfall here. The process we're recommending is not therapy; it's problem solving. Emotions are a problem, not a solution. Do not use your ally as a psychotherapist.

This isn't to say that there's no value to processing your emotions or finding causes for your inefficiencies in old trauma or disappointments. Far from it—for many people such a process can be extremely useful. We're just saying this isn't the time for it.

When you've got your time commitments under control, you may wish to consider allocating some of your attention to personal recovery and growth. But when you're in crisis, you need to avoid adding extra commitments. Wait until the crisis is resolved before you try processing your emotional difficulties.

also lead to overconfidence, which can lead into the downward spiral of overcommitment. Be proud of yourself for doing something well, but keep your pride under control and realistic or it may come back to bite you.

In general, emotions should be kept in check in the workplace. In particular, if you're feeling shame, begin by forgiving yourself. Promise yourself to do better in the future, but don't make that promise until you've genuinely forgiven yourself.

Forgive Your Bosses and Your Customers

After you've forgiven yourself, forgive those around you. Your bosses, employees, customers, and constituents all have pressures and needs of their own to which they're responding. Don't carry a grudge.

Get Organized

A good way to break out of a negative emotional state is to take the time to get organized.

When you feel overwhelmed, you don't want to get into a complete office remodel. But on the other hand, we often find that people who feel overwhelmed are surrounded by a paperwork salad where notes and documents relating to all their responsibilities are mixed together.

Taking a little time to sort out this salad can pay off fairly quickly in both time and stress. What's more, the visible change can lift your spirits.

This doesn't mean that you should tolerate excessive demands in the future. One of the advantages of having a clear inventory of responsibilities is that it helps you deal with those who are encouraging you to take on too much. Say, "Here is what I am doing already. This takes me at least 50 hours a week, and I'm unable to do more than that. Which activity would you like me to curtail or drop to make room for your new demand?"

Occasionally, you will run into top brass who believe that it's always possible to get a little bit more out of people. We encountered one such person at a state agency where we delivered a lecture. Our interviews with staff led us to believe that the demands and stresses of the place were far beyond tolerable levels, and we offered exactly the advice of the previous paragraph. We were embarrassed to find the head of the agency present. Astonishingly, though, he said that he'd enjoyed our presentation and totally missed any implied criticism of the management style. He used the words "always possible to get a little more out of people." This assertion is obviously factually wrong; otherwise, each person would be capable of an infinite amount of work. Nevertheless, he said it with a straight face.

If you find yourself in an organization with such a person above you, our advice is to seek a way out. In the meantime, you'll have to make the decisions as to which of your unrealistic load of responsibilities to ignore or curtail. Even so, don't be angry. Your boss, though capable of believing something transparently impossible, probably means well. A tolerant attitude will reduce your stress level substantially while you plan your escape.

By the way, if you're in the private sector and your customers are placing too many demands upon you, that's good news, not bad. Raise your prices.

The Promised Land of Slack

As a manager, it's absolutely essential to keep a certain amount of time uncommitted if you're to do your job properly.

Your job doesn't just entail fulfilling all your commitments and taking on a reasonable stream of commitments in the future. It also involves identifying and solving problems, conveying the concerns of the production staff to upper management and those of upper management to your staff, and proposing and implementing new initiatives.

In particular, as you work through this book looking for ways to get a better grip on those projects you and your team are working on, you'll need free time to plan and implement your initiatives. An analogy may clarify this. When you accept delivery of a new sofa, you should have removed the old one already. You need to make room for new initiatives in your calendar just as you need to clear floor space for new furniture.

This means that your goal is to have a calendar that's not just keeping you from being overloaded, but allowing you a certain amount of freedom as well. Allow yourself to imagine how much more fun your work will be when that becomes possible. Use that image to motivate yourself through your difficulties.

Make Room

Make space for the changes you want to take place!
Every new initiative requires time for planning and implementation. Make room on your calendar for new initiatives, enough time to do them right. It makes no sense to take a good idea and condemn it to mediocre results or even failure because you don't allocate enough time for it.

Addressing the Problem

You've now done something substantive: you now have a clear idea of how overcommitted you are. That should give you reason to be at least a little optimistic. It means that you have a specific goal.

Unfortunately, that's a new goal, in addition to all the other ones! However, it won't take much time, just careful thought. Your goal is to look at all of your commitments and identify how you're going to cope.

There are basically two ways to address overcommitment. You can increase output or you can decrease demands. You must do one or both of these. Otherwise, you'll fail to deliver on some of your commitments.

Here are the ways to increase output:

- Get help (delegate or outsource)
- Work the right number of hours
- Increase efficiency

Here are the ways to decrease demand:

- Delay
- Get less fussy
- Partial delivery
- Drop some work

Delegating and Outsourcing

The simplest way to get out of a crunch is go get help.

Of course, delegating and outsourcing are possible only in certain situations. Some tasks are too closely associated with your own work to hand off. It's possible that you may not have the funds to support outsourcing some of your work. Finally, subordinates to whom you may wish to delegate may be just as busy with the current crunch as you.

On the other hand, it's easy to miss opportunities to delegate by thinking too narrowly. Perhaps no one but you can complete that technical report that's due in two weeks. Try to find some other part of your workload that you can delegate to an assistant. Be creative.

Can you delegate some other part of your life? Can you send the kids off to Grandma's for a couple of weeks? Can you ask a friend who owes you a favor to mow the lawn? Delegating aspects of your personal life can free up time for unusual work commitments. Of course, such tactics should only be used rarely!

There's a lot to delegating effectively, which we'll discuss in some detail in later chapters. If this option is available to you, it's the best way to reduce your load in a crunch.

Changing Your Hours

You could, of course, work more hours. As we've already mentioned, this doesn't guarantee that you'll get more done. There's some level of work beyond which the marginal value of each additional hour is negative: the more hours you work, the less you'll get done. Assuming you're nowhere near that point, if you can free up time to work more hours temporarily, that's a possibility worth considering.

However, if you're already tired, you need to account for the fact that each additional hour is worth less than a full hour in any case. For instance, the 40th through 60th hours may be worth only 10 effective hours. You also need to be very careful not to allow this strategy to become a regular disruption of your personal life.

If you're working much too hard, you may actually find that you get more done if you work fewer hours.

Increasing Your Efficiency

Another way to increase your output is to become more efficient.

In a crunch, effective increases in efficiency must require only a small time investment and produce an immediate return. Many ways to increase efficiency are possible in the long run, but this is not the time to be considering them.

There are two suggestions that we frequently make to customers at this stage.

The first is a straightforward organization of documents in your workspace. We've mentioned the "paper salad" of documents that people in a work crunch often generate in their workspace. This can cause a lot of stress and waste a lot of time.

Don't aim at reorganizing your office completely at this point. But it's possible to look at a surprising number of documents in a short time if you're making simple decisions about them.

Depending on the mess and the time available, you could use the technique we described in Chapter 1. Look at each document for just one second. Sort the documents into five piles: current business, important archives, trash, items to be routed, and uncertain. Dump the trash pile. Pass along the documents to be routed. Set the archive items aside, to be filed later. Put the uncertain items into a box, out of the way. That way, you've got only the current business documents, which you should group according to the active projects.

There's a simpler version of this technique. Make a pile of documents that should be immediately routed. Make a pile of documents for each active project. Put aside any papers that don't require routing and aren't relevant to active projects. This effort can pay off quite quickly—it's a real time-saver. More to the point, it greatly decreases stress when you're able to put your hands on what you need when you need it. This reduction of stress pays back in efficiency.

A second approach that works in some situations is to "batch" similar activities. This approach is particularly useful in response to "thrashing," the sort of paralysis that arises from having too many things to do. The idea is to clearly divide your schedule into various pursuits. If something that you aren't currently working on pops into your mind, you can then make a note of it on the appropriate list and tell yourself something like "I've scheduled time to deal with that sort of thing on Thursday." This clears your attention to work on your current task.

> **Key Term**
>
> **Batch** To group tasks for more efficient handling. We borrow this term from computer science, where it's defined as "to group sets of data or jobs, each set to be processed in a single program run." When you group activities by category, you're using a batching strategy to increase your efficiency.

You can batch by function (return phone calls during one period, answer correspondence during another) or by project. It can be very helpful to allocate hours in your busy weeks to specific pursuits. This can both improve concentration and reduce uncertainty about what activity to pursue next. A very modest amount of planning, both daily and weekly, can dramatically improve your effectiveness when you're dealing with a large number of activities (more about this in Chapter 10).

A related problem that can exacerbate overload stress is difficulty in concentrating. Some people who have certain free-wheeling mental styles can be categorized as "very creative" in some situations and "attention deficit disordered" in others. The sheer quantity of items you need to deal with can combine with stress to make concentration harder than ever.

If you find yourself in this circumstance, you can recover much of your lost creativity with the simple expedient of a digital timer. Set a timer for a brief amount of time (maybe five minutes at first) and face the counter away from you. Then, when the timer beeps, make a note of whether you had drifted off the topic at hand or were working. If you maintain your focus three times in a row, increase the amount of time, gradually reaching a half hour or so.

Negotiating Delay or Partial Delivery

You may find that you can resolve your workload problem by becoming more efficient and delegating better. If so, you're fortunate. Congratulations!

It's likely, though, that these steps won't be enough. That's when it's time to face facts and decide which ambitions to abandon.

Negotiated delay or partial delivery is the least painful option. Perhaps some of your deadlines are not as firm as you had been led to believe. Discuss this with the recipients of your work. If necessary, offer some compensation for your lateness.

It's often the case that customers set deadlines that are very conservative for them. So it could be that one of the deadlines that you're working the hardest to meet is less important to the customer than you think. Perhaps the customer's situation has changed so your work is no longer on the critical path for their next delivery. Ask around to see which of your deadlines can be shifted. If you're in a position to offer incentives to some of your customers, consider doing so, whether this is a reduction in price or an offer of extra value added if they permit a delay.

The sooner you seek an alternative of this sort, the more likely you can find one. This is not a pleasant negotiation, but it can be the one you need to move you from the impossible to the merely difficult.

Avoiding Unnecessary Perfectionism

Oftentimes, you'll find yourself working to standards that matter more to you than to your customer. In those cases, it may well pay to become less of a perfectionist. If there's a delivery that's acceptable to the customer but not to you, that's still much better than the other way around. See if there are corners you can cut that would not offend your customer or compromise your ethics. If your pride suffers a little, it's a small price to pay for easing your workload.

Abandoning the Right Item

If you've gone through all of the above options and still not found a way to get your scheduled deliveries to be realistic, you must abandon at least one of your projects.

We frequently get to this point with our customers, and they often resist this tactic. But you've got to face facts. After all, when you've examined every other alternative, this is all that's left. One of our figurative restaurant customers will never receive his figurative cheeseburger. Now, we've got to decide which one.

To make this difficult decision, list all active projects and identify the consequences of abandoning each of them. Try to assign a number to each, in terms of an intuitive consequence or a pure dollar amount. Then find the project or set of projects that, if abandoned, would free up enough hours to make your workload realistic with the least negative consequences.

Then 'fess up and face the music. Call your contacts on each of the projects you're cutting and tell them that you've erred, and you won't be able to complete the work. Take whatever consequences ensue.

If it's going to be necessary to drop an item, the sooner you do so, the better. Hanging on to an unfeasible delivery will just add to your load and your stress, without any payoff.

Failing

Failure is the worst possible outcome. It essentially has all the bad features of unilaterally abandoning a task—and then some. Your customer will be angrier with you for an unannounced failure than for an apologetic abandonment. The failed project will have taken time, energy, and resources away from other endeavors, hurting your performance on all of them without providing any returns.

> ### Now, Play It Smart and Safe
>
> Well, the exercise was successful and you found a reasonable path out of your work crunch.
>
> Now, suddenly, a golden opportunity comes along. Unfortunately, it will take some time before you emerge from your crunch of very tight deadlines.
>
> Think very carefully about the opportunity. If you cannot resist pursuing it, you'll need to go through the whole exercise again. Try to avoid any new commitments until you emerge from the crunch period.

It's much better to drop a task deliberately than to try very hard and fail at the last minute. When you know you're overloaded, don't try to fool yourself and others into believing that all is OK.

Some people seem to feel that it's heroic to pursue a project when there's no hope of success. No, it's really not heroic. It's basically an ego trip, because it causes problems for others, directly and indirectly, and nobody benefits except the person who needs to feel heroic.

Sustainability

When you finally emerge from your crunch, you'll probably find yourself in a secondary crunch of work you were putting off during the primary crunch. Don't despair. Keep an eye on your commitment levels, using the methods of the last chapter, and adjust as necessary, using the methods described here. Workload management is a central task of a manager and this activity will be ongoing.

Still, keep in mind that to be reliable you need to avoid workload crises. A typical manager should aim to keep no more than 80% or 85% committed, to allow for time to be creative and time to deal with unexpected events.

It's when you can consistently maintain a level of free attention that you can most effectively improve your own productivity and take advantage of the suggestions in the remainder of the book to improve the productivity of your group. Remember that planning is a major part of your work, so be sure to allow for it in your time budget.

Manager's Checklist for Chapter 6

❏ It's important to know exactly how overloaded you are, in order to develop effective strategies to get the overload under control.

❏ Knowing you're overloaded can be very discouraging. Addressing this discouragement can be important in recovering from overload.

❏ Shame is an emotion that comes easily when you're over-committed, but it's not very helpful. Your natural tendency to elicit shame when others disappoint you or to feel it when you disappoint others must be minimized. Forgive yourself and those around you, then get on with your recovery strategies.

❏ To get out from under a work crunch, consider the following:
  • Delegate and outsource.
  • Work more hours temporarily.
  • Implement simple changes to increase your efficiency.

❏ Avoid new commitments until you emerge from your overload.

❏ To manage effectively, any manager must have a certain amount of uncommitted time. Aim to commit no more than 80% or 85% of your time, to allow for unexpected events and new initiatives that arise.

Group Time Management: "As Simple as Possible, but No Simpler"

Everything should be made as simple as possible, but no simpler.

—Albert Einstein

It's a bit long for a book title, but "allocating the efforts of several people to accomplish multiple responsibilities" is an important part of what this book is about. In short, we're expanding the ideas of time management to the group. In this chapter, we'll look for the ways in which the group management problem extends the ideas of conventional time management and the crisis-recovery ideas that we presented in the previous two chapters.

Make Room for Change in Yourself

We recommend that you complete the personal inventory exercise in Chapter 5 and, if necessary, incorporate the recovery strategies in Chapter 6 before you attempt to implement the measures suggested in this and subsequent chapters. There are two reasons for this.

First, the actions needed to improve a group's performance require careful attention both to technical details and to interpersonal interactions. A manager should never take on improving group performance as an afterthought or, even worse, in the heat of frustration and chaos.

Second, there's the matter of setting a good example. There's nothing so futile as a disorganized manager striving to have an organized team. Most staff members perceive that as hypocritical. What's more, any increases in systematization will be perceived as not being a serious commitment on the part of management.

"Physician, heal thyself!" Recover first, then improve. You don't take on a new athletic activity while you have the flu. Don't take on a new work initiative when your system is stressed.

Setting an Example

Remember that as a manager you're in a leadership role. If you aren't managing your own time effectively, you'll have a great deal of difficulty getting the authority to manage others' time.

Leading by Example

We consulted with a regional purchasing manager who was very dissatisfied with the reliability of his office support. On a regular basis, tasks were being dropped or barely rescued in a last-minute adrenalin rush.

As we got to know him, we discovered that he was deeply disorganized. He was a classic case of the responsible person with no time management skills. His task-tracking method was sticky notes on the monitor, his filing system was piles on his desktop, and his appointment calendar was entirely in his brain. Rather than dealing with his staff, we insisted on focusing on the manager.

As we got his problems under control, his office suddenly became a much more pleasant environment and staff members expressed enthusiasm and amazement. They began to ask for similar assistance. Had the boss demanded better organization while he remained disorganized, the staff would have found it insincere and rude. Instead, the boss got organized, and the staff actually asked for similar assistance. The needed change met with enthusiasm, rather than resistance.

It's rare that a manager is unfamiliar with personal time management techniques, but if you are, it's essential that you firmly understand and use this material before you try to implement changes in the activities of your workgroup.

Once you know how to manage your own time and are doing so well enough that you have some extra energy to devote to seeing the big picture, you can begin looking for ways to improve the workflow of your group.

Like any skill—driving a car, hitting a baseball, or playing the piano—time management is awkward at first but becomes progressively easier. The problem is that when your motivation is strongest is the time when the mental energy you have available for it is lowest.

If you've been following along in the previous chapters, you now have a systematic way to evaluate whether or not you're in a personal workflow crisis and, if so, you have ideas for escaping from the crisis.

Though crisis recovery is a neglected corner of time management, we've found it absolutely essential, in both its technical and its emotional components, in making progress with most of our clients, who generally call upon our services when they're in some trouble. Normal time management techniques fail utterly in a crisis situation—and yet that's when many people try to implement them. They end up discouraged, believing that they're inherently incapable of behaving systematically.

Make Room for Change in the Group

In this chapter, we'll work on identifying what a sustainable group time management system might look like. Please don't rush to put these plans into place, though. You'll need to manage the time and pace of implementation. Think of the next three chapters as a unit to study. We'll need to move carefully to do this right.

Extensions of Time Management

If time management can be defined as getting the most out of yourself, is project management defined as getting the most out of your group? This is not the usual meaning of project management at all. The usual definition of the art of project management is the endeavor of bringing together multiple human and capital resources to achieve a goal to specification, on time, and within budget.

Many project managers are the lead for a single large project at a time. This can be a daunting responsibility for extremely large and high-visibility projects. Still, the project manager in this case has a single, well-defined goal and advocates for it.

If you're reading this book, on the other hand, you're likely managing a fixed team across multiple projects and objectives, so you want sustained thriving rather than a single, large success. Doing so is an extension of time management to the group.

Managing the attention of a group of, say, seven people is, in principle, at least seven times as complicated as managing the attention of a single person. In fact, it's usually more complicated than that. This is because there are ways in which the efforts of the group can be traded off among members, activities that one person can perform as well as another. These possibilities can help you solve your problem, but they also present more variables to track. There are also issues of how projects are passed from one person to another, how often and for what reason meetings are useful, and how extra effort can be avoided in the collaborative process.

Extending the To-Do List to the Group

Our purpose is to create a reliable group. To do so, we need to form a clear idea of the commitments of the group. This may or may not be an explicit list, though in principle it's probably a good idea if it can be made explicit. What's absolutely necessary, though, is to account for the group's commitments in such a way that each commitment is clear and not easily misunderstood by the person to whom the commitment is made.

At a commercial establishment that deals with the public, these commitments are usually perfectly clear. To go back to our original example, a customer typically knows that he's ordered a cheeseburger, and you've confirmed it by accepting his order (and possibly his money).

Commitments made to other groups within a large organization are sometimes less clear. Did the engineers promise to do a feasibility study or did they simply state how long such a study would take? Is "I can have it for you in two weeks" the same as "I will have it for you in two weeks"? Similarly, have you made offhand comments that others might take as commitments?

A formal procedure for promising things within an organization can be helpful, not only for tracking commitments, but also simply for identifying what commitments are made.

Making an explicit list of commitments can be troublesome if there are many small items to track. As we take our group workload inventory, we will require an estimate of the commitment load from each person or, at the very least, from each person who claims to be working near his or her capacity.

Who's Promising What to Whom by When?

Smart Managing

Commitments made on behalf of a work group within an organization can be difficult for the group's manager to track. If you have this problem, consider instituting a formal procedure for tracking promises. Your system should identify what commitments have been made, including due dates and an estimate of the resources required.

Staying out of Trouble in the Future

It's your job as manager of the group to ensure that the group does not make more commitments than it can handle. This is the equivalent of the time management planning phase when you move items from your master list to your calendar.

In some situations, a manager can control the flow of work. If a manager doesn't have direct control, he or she must look for more long-term solutions. One way a manager can control the flow is by negotiating the due date, saying something like "Yes, you can have the Blossom Proposal, but not until two weeks from Friday." In other situations, the manager cannot directly control the due dates and labor required for commitments made. In that case, it's necessary to find indirect ways to control the quantity of work. Changes to pricing and incentives or hiring and laying off staff are ways to match work commitments to staff availability.

In any case, it is the manager's job to match the workload with the available resources. To do this, you must begin with a realistic assessment of the workload and the resources that you maintain constantly.

Extending the Calendar to the Group

Moving items from the to-do list to the calendar is the crux of the problem in managing the time of a group. The obvious problem is that the calendar is a much more complicated structure for a group than for an individual.

If you're keeping track of what you yourself are doing, you simply have 24 hours in a day to allocate to this or that. If you followed our exercise in Chapter 5, you have some idea whether you have enough hours or not, so it's just a matter of allocating those hours.

For your group, of course, there are several people who can be doing things on any given day. It may sometimes be obvious who is to do what, but sometimes it will not be so obvious.

In fact, although each individual should have a single official calendar allocating his or her own time and should never have two, in a sense a group always has two calendars.

On each day, there's a group of people whose time may or may not be assigned for each time slot. This is the *personnel-view calendar*. On the other hand, on each day there's a group of active projects that may or may not be assigned to someone. This is the *project-view calendar*. Depending on the nature of the work you do, one or the other of these calendars may be most important, but both will always be present as soon as more than one person is working on more than one project.

Effective management of multiple projects requires skill at moving items around on these calendars. Sometimes this isn't

---

Specialized Calendars

Two tools are critical to time management for a group: the personnel-view calendar and the project-view calendar. Both views draw from the same set of information about people and commitments, but order that information in different ways.

The personnel-view calendar is a list of people in your workgroup, with each name followed by that individual's commitments, deadlines, and time estimates.

The project-view calendar is a list of commitments, with each commitment followed by the name of the individual assigned to it and other relevant information such as deadlines and time estimates.

Your unassigned commitments should appear at the top of the project-view calendar, so that no commitment can fall through the cracks. Your busiest people should appear at the top of the personnel-view calendar, since they require more attention to scheduling to avoid bottlenecks.

---

difficult; sometimes it's a tremendous challenge. So, let's start with the simplest cases.

As Simple as Possible

There are two extreme cases where group time management is not at all substantially different from individual time management.

In one such extreme, each project is handled by an individual team member and the necessary equipment is sufficiently available.

Reporters are close to this ideal. Each reporter works an assigned beat, such as sports or finance. Whether one reporter is ahead or behind, overworked or underchallenged, has little effect on the activities of any other reporter. The editor (the workgroup's manager) needs to keep close track of who's doing what, but each individual reporter is a separate and independent management problem.

Whether such a team can manage its load depends only on whether the individual members of the team are too busy. Your role as traffic cop amounts mostly to participating in the decision of which jobs to pursue and to whom to assign them as they come in. Getting clear answers from people about where they stand on the work is just a matter of getting to know the individuals, how they report their status, and how that relates to prior work history.

The other extreme is where team members are perfectly inter-changeable. This usually occurs with low-skilled work, where any worker can fill any role. A team of cashiers is a perfect example. Planning for such a team is simply a matter of matching available hours with work demands. In other words, the entire team can be treated as a single time management problem.

Suppose you have seven people, each working an eight-hour day. Your problem is not much different from managing a single person who works a 56-hour day. Whether your group is overloaded or not depends only on whether you have more than 56 hours of work to do on a given day, nothing else. Your job amounts to finding as close to 56 hours of productive work to do as possible, without going over.

Using the Personnel Calendar

In practice, things are rarely as simple as in our two extreme situations. However, in many situations there's a simplifying assumption that can greatly help in your planning. This is to identify your most critical resource.

In industrial situations, this is typically a critical piece of pro-duction machinery that's the limiting factor. In that case, the manager's job is primarily to optimize the performance of that particular machine, since it determines the output of the whole operation. Meanwhile, the manager should be looking to increase the capacity of the line, by upgrading the machine or getting a second one.

In service operations, the situation is not always quite so clear. People, unlike machines, will do what they can to appear indispensable, whether they are or not. However, as a manager you'll probably have a good idea how important various people are to your operation. While it may trouble your sense of egali-tarianism, it might be a good idea to identify which team mem-ber is the bottleneck in your operation.

Oddly, there are two opposite reasons why someone is a bottleneck. It can be because the person performs tasks slowly or because the person has talents that are in high demand and are hard to replicate. It's also possible that the bottleneck person or machine in your operation changes with the season or the marketplace or other external considerations.

In any case, after you've identified the critical resource of your operation, you should begin your scheduling with that person. He or she should be given only tasks that no one else can do (to the extent that morale will allow). Even if this person can do other tasks better than other team members, you should allocate first the tasks that no one else can do.

Proceed from your highest-demand person to your next highest and so on down the line, allocating the most difficult tasks first. If, as you do this, you still end up with consistent delays at these points in the pipeline, you should look for additional resources in these areas.

Using the Project Calendar

We've just completed the bottleneck-first method of assigning people to projects. Hopefully, you can juggle your assignments so that deadline-driven projects can all be done on time. This won't always work on the first pass.

What if your critical staff member is the only person who can do job A, but is also the fastest at doing job B? What if job B is on a tight deadline? In this case, the methods that best allocate people to tasks for total throughput are not the same as the methods required to achieve delivery on a par-

> **Throughput** The output or production resulting from a specific resource (such as an individual or machine) over a period of time.

Key Term

ticular project. Of course, this is just the simplest case. In the real world, several projects, people, and skills may be involved.

The single-minded, conventional single-project manager does not have this problem. That problem is dominated by the project

Critical path The series of consecutive activities that represent the longest path through a multithreaded project. The importance of knowing and tracking the critical path is that any activity on the critical path that falls behind schedule by one day will directly delay the project end date by one day.

calendar, which is elaborated to show various critical paths and timings. The competition among individual projects is not crucial in that situation, so the personnel view of the calendar is less important.

There's no easy solution. With a computer and with perfect predictability of tasks and skills, it would be possible to do an exhaustive search of all possible assignments. Usually, though, the situation isn't so marginal that if a solution exists you won't be able to find it.

Your strategy depends on whether you're driven by deadlines or by throughput. If by throughput, focus on the personnel view, with the critical personnel as your focus of attention. If by deadlines, focus on the project view, with your attention on the most challenging deliveries.

Signs: Throughput vs. Timing

A manager in a sign shop is responsible for scheduling jobs. He finds that the laminating machine is the point at which most bottlenecks in sign production occur. Why? In this situation the demands of throughput and of timing are in conflict.

For most efficient throughput, the various sign jobs must be grouped by the type of lamination required: some signs get a high-gloss coating, others a special fade-resistant coating, and so on.

For fastest delivery, the jobs must be grouped by due date rather than by type of lamination. This significantly slows down the throughput, because changing over from one coating to another takes about 20 minutes.

For this manager, the answer lies in negotiating sufficient turnaround times on sign orders to allow for the most cost-efficient scheduling strategy—one that maximizes throughput rather than speed.

Complications of Time Management

You can see that time management, although a good starting point for group management, can be quite a bit more of a puzzle. There are other complicating factors that we haven't mentioned yet.

The fewer complicating factors, the simpler your strategy can be and still be effective. Complexity in a strategy leads to additional overhead and risk of failure. Like a mechanical engineer, you should strive for a strategy that does the job with the fewest moving parts.

Let's consider some of the complicating factors.

Visibility

In managing your own time, you have a clear idea of how well your actual activity has matched your plans and you can work on improving the match between plan and outcomes. In managing the activities of a group, on the other hand, knowing exactly what happened and why can be problematic. Also, as team leader, it's part of your job to respond to questions about the status of any item for which you've taken responsibility.

One extra component of team time management, then, is obtaining accurate information about what's happening. We'll be discussing this in detail in the next chapter.

Fungibility

In planning your own time, you may wish to put your most demanding tasks at the time of day when you're most effective, whatever your habits and physiology suggest. If you do this, you're treating your own hours as not fungible, not interchangeable in a simple way.

The extension of this principle to your team can be a significant complicating factor. If there's no fungibility at all, your team is inflexible and at a disadvantage, but assigning people to tasks is relatively straightforward. On the other hand, if there are various task types and various skill levels, the problem of assigning people to tasks becomes much more complicated.

Fungibility Interchangeability of resources. A resource is fungible if a similar resource can be substituted for it without consequence.

The term originates in commodities trading. Graded wheat is fungible: one shipment of a specific grade can be substituted for another. Fine wine is not fungible: the customers are quite particular as to the origin and vintage of each bottle.

A fungible human resource is a person who's working on an activity to which it would be easy to assign another person. The more fungible activities your team has, the more flexibility you have in making assignments.

A management theory called the theory of constraints, promoted by Eli Goldratt, is very helpful in addressing this question. The theory was worked out in manufacturing plants, but it applies equally to service teams. The central point is that there's typically a single limiting factor in the productivity of any system and almost always a very small number of such limiting factors, or constraints. The constraint may be effective use of a piece of equipment or maximum billability of a particular team member.

If there's a key member of your team, your objective should be to keep that team member doing the critical work as much as possible. If there are portions of that person's workload that can be transferred to someone else, then do so.

The simplest approach to multiple capacities is to honestly focus first on the member of the team (or piece of equipment) most critical to the overall performance of the group. Once you've allocated that person's time, move on to the next most critical.

Smart Managing

First Schedule the Person in Greatest Demand

A way to simplify the allocation of multiple people to multiple projects is to begin by focusing first on your person with the highest ratio of demand-to-availability. Order the tasks to be assigned by how critical that staff member is to each task's completion. Assign the most critical tasks first and proceed in descending order until all the work is allocated.

Threadability

We discussed the possibility of multithreaded projects in Chapter 4. As you recall, multithreading is having more than one part of a project proceeding at one time.

You need to decide whether the group as a whole should support multithreading. The main advantage is that, if done correctly, it reduces the wall-clock or calendar time for a given project. The overall work for the team, though, generally increases. If few of your products are time-critical in this way, it may not be worth the effort to support multithreading.

If you do support multithreading, you'll need to identify the projects that can be multithreaded, define the individual threads and the way to make sure they come together, and allocate roles to each thread. We'll discuss this in more detail in Chapter 11.

Granularity

By granularity, we mean the extent to which a project can be broken down into separate tasks. It's a question of duration and workload. How long will a project take? How much work is required? How many tasks will it involve? How long will each task take? How much work will there be in each task?

Your projects may be of a typical duration and workload or they may span a wide range from short duration to long duration and from light workload to heavy workload. A wide range indicates a diverse granularity—definitely more challenging to manage. If the challenge becomes too great, especially if it strains the members of your group, consider letting go of projects that are too far out of your typical range.

A team with smaller projects has less need for formal tracking, because it's easier to remember the status of each project and

> **Key Term**
>
> **Granularity** The extent to which a project consists of separate components. The greater the granularity of a project, the more components, so management of the project can be more flexible. However, when projects differ widely in terms of duration and/or workload, managing them becomes more difficult.

Recognize Your Limits

Most managers are ambitious; they have a positive attitude, a "can do" approach to their work. That's great—usually.

However, it can also cause problems. If your projects vary too much in granularity, the challenge of managing them may be more than it's worth, especially if the resulting schedules overwhelm, confuse, or frustrate the members of your group. If so, consider ways to limit the range of the projects that you take on.

its workflow, and less tolerance for formal tracking, because the same overhead task is a larger proportion of the total effort. Such fine granularity of projects is relatively easy to manage.

The most complicated case arises where the team has both small and large projects—a wide range of granularity, in other words. The large projects cannot be managed using the simple methods appropriate to smaller ones, while the smaller projects cannot tolerate the overhead appropriate to larger ones. One approach is to formalize this distinction between large and small and to have two or more types of projects, each with its own strategy, but this can be complicated.

The size of the individual tasks also affects planning.

You Need Talent and Systems

A printing firm had several talented young artists doing layout work for clients. Senior management decided to take advantage of the situation, by advertising the art staff as a graphic design studio. New, larger projects came in, but the work did not flow as smoothly as management would have liked. Why?

The work group had the talent, but not the organizational systems, to handle the larger projects. As the granularity of the projects increased, so did the difficulty in knowing what to work on when. The group's manager soon instituted a system to identify and track short-term and long-term projects, and an approach to assigning the graphic artists, so that one team tackled the larger projects and the other handled the day-to-day layout work. Occasional rotation between the teams increased the variety of each individual's workday and ensured that every artist gained experience with each type of project.

Avoid Interrupting High-Value Personnel

People whose concentrated efforts are central to your mission should be interrupted as seldom as possible. One way to achieve this is to schedule their meetings at the beginning or end of the day.

The manager should flex his or her schedule to meet the needs of high-value production staff, rather than the other way around. One way to approach such staff is to send an e-mail saying such as, "Please drop by my office when you reach a good stopping point." Your job is to reduce their distractions, not add to them.

Projects made up of larger tasks present more difficulties to the planning process. Tasks that are of a long duration and don't split well require intense concentration. Staff members who typically have longer tasks should be scheduled very carefully. Try to keep their meetings toward the beginning or end of the day and the week.

Predictability

Is there a steady stream of work? Or does it come in irregularly, unpredictably? Work that's not predictable is much more disruptive than work that's predictable. That doesn't surprise you, of course. But you should think about the implications of that common-sense observation.

One implication is that you should be careful about combining tasks. Consider what each task involves.

Here's an example. Very often, small businesses feel compelled to combine reception and accounting functions into a single job. That's a mistake, because these work types are extremely incompatible. Reception tasks are utterly unpredictable and should not be combined with tasks that require concentration.

Losing one's place in an accounting task can be very costly and may cause long-term damage to a business. That's a heavy price to pay for answering one phone call. A person immersed in figures trying to track a financial problem cannot be expected to switch hats immediately when the phone rings or a visitor arrives and handle the interruption pleasantly and attentively. One contact handled less than appropriately can be one too many.

If possible, small businesses or work groups should team up and share a receptionist and have somebody else do the accounting. Generally, persons on high interrupt should be regarded as having limited availability for production work.

The biggest impact on planning, though, is the predictability of the overall workload. Does your business need excess capacity to handle peak demand? The electric utility company isn't in a good position to turn away business when it is busy. Are you? If not, and if your work is variable and hard to predict, you'll need to provide excess capacity just as the electric utility does.

You'll also want to devise procedures and techniques for making the best use of slack, as we discussed in Chapters 4 and 5 and will cover in Chapter 8.

Manager's Checklist for Chapter 7

❑ Set a good example. Put in place the strategies you need for good personal time management before you take on improving your group's performance.

❑ The types of information you use to manage your own time—the to-do list and the calendar—are equally critical in managing multiple projects and multiple people. How you use this information will depend on what's more important to your operations—meeting deadlines or maximizing throughput.

❑ Group time management is different from personal time management in that interpersonal issues come into play. These include your need for an accurate assessment of the levels of skill and availability for each member of your group and your need for a degree of control over what each member is doing at any given time.

❑ Group time commitments can be viewed by project or by person. In many situations, it's worthwhile to keep in mind both ways of looking at commitments. The project calendar is more important in an operation driven by deadlines, while the personnel calendar is more important in a situation where throughput is more important than promptness.

❑ Both the size of the project and the size of individual tasks can be important in how you run your operation. The larger the variation, the more difficult the management problem. Consider letting go of projects that are too far out of your typical range.

Getting the Big Picture: Commitments and the Team

Nobody expects an electric power plant to operate at 100% of capacity at all times. The capacity of the plant is designed to deal with peak loads. There is no way to force the utility's customers to keep their demands at exactly the same level at all times. The very idea is ridiculous. We expect the utility to pay the price of maintaining a capacity that matches the highest level of demand we'll place upon it.

Yet this ridiculous idea is applied to workgroups all the time.

The Paradox of Slack

The idea of constant demand is an extension of the early industrial assembly line. In an assembly line setting, most jobs are low-skilled, so a manager can easily assign any line worker to any position. When such a factory is active, each of the line workers must keep up with the line and each of the line positions must be filled. The manager should fill any empty positions quickly, but should send home any extra hands immediately.

Most of our workplaces are more like a utility than like an old factory. We don't have a huge number of hands to assign to share the workload, and we can't easily lay off or add staff. Our staff is more like a productive capacity to be maintained than like an inventory of labor to be tapped.

In high-value service settings, workloads change according to outside conditions beyond our control. The larger corporate or social context expects us to be able to handle peak capacity. Logically, then, we should tolerate some inefficiency in allocating our workers to billable tasks, all the more so when our work is more variable and less predictable.

Yet, most workplaces structure their time reporting just like an assembly line. There's an expectation that each person will report exactly 35 or exactly 40 hours of work per week.

Most of us enjoy taking breaks or loafing, studying and learning new skills, or bonding with fellow employees. Yet most workers in most environments feel guilty when they're "caught" in such slack activities.

Other employees work far more than their allotment, but regularly fail to report that time. (In our town, this is actually the universal practice among school principals, for example.) Finding that normal working hours don't suffice to cover their job descriptions, they work after hours or on weekends to fulfill their obligations, yet fail to report this time.

The Polish author Stanislaw Lem once wrote a light science fiction story that was actually a sly critique of the oppressive Soviet communist regime of the time. In that story, a society held the ideology that the highest form of life was the fish and that people could train themselves to be more like fish. Breathing air was illegal in this society. Of course, the basic idea being impossible, everyone was constantly sneaking out of sight for a breath of air and ignoring everyone else doing so. Demanding that everyone in a professional workplace be doing billable work at all times is as unrealistic an ideology as the one in the story that required everyone to develop gills.

Part of your job as a manager is to cut through all this fiction and get to the truth. Allocating people's time and attention requires that you understand how the demands of their positions are translated into behavior.

Approaching 100 Percent

Consider what's happening if all members of your production staff are completely busy all the time. Unless each person works independently of all others, there will be some bottleneck, some person whose performance limits the output of the entire system. It may seem like a good idea to keep everyone else busy while this is happening, but you need to be very careful in such cases not to add work that affects the limiting resource.

The typical case, if everyone is busy and their work is interconnected, is that there's an ever-increasing backlog at the slower points in the system. In other words, in the long run your performance must be based on the slowest points in the system. Consequently, anyone who isn't at such a point can be expected to have some free time.

Of course, getting the most out of your people is exactly our purpose here. Even though excess capacity is necessary, it's costly. You therefore have two objectives. First, you need to limit excess capacity as much as possible. Look for activities that make more use of the less critical people in proportion to those in high demand. Second, make the best possible use of the excess capacity that still remains. Often, the best use is to train those members of the group in the skills that are critical for the business, so that they're able to handle a wider range of tasks, making managing easier and reducing constraints in your system.

By the way, the ideas in this section owe much to the book we mentioned

MISTAKE PROOFING

Split Your Slacks

Slack time can be split between formal self-improvement and informal morale-building, as it suits the group and the circumstances. Let your group know how you think slack time should be spent. Some members of your group might have some specific ideas that they should share with the others.

> ### Work with Assignments ... and with Attitudes
> The extent of utilization of your team is determined by the person or other resource most likely to hold up production. You can improve your overall efficiency by offloading work from that person or resource or by changing your workload to favor demands on other resources.
>
> It's important to be realistic, though. Not everyone will be busy all the time. If your workplace culture doesn't allow people to admit that, it will make your job harder, because you'll have to determine who's working very hard and who's trying to look busy. While it's true that some people try to look busy because they're lazy or somehow incapacitated, others look busy because they don't have enough work and don't want to admit it. Understand that repairing this situation is part of your responsibility as a manager.

earlier by Tom DeMarco, *Slack: Getting Past Burnout, Busywork, and the Myth of Total Efficiency* (New York: Broadway Books, 2001). There's much more to this paradoxical topic than we can cover here, and we recommend this and DeMarco's other books highly.

Interviewing Skills

Identifying the constraint in your system is critical to your job as traffic cop. You must identify the key place or places where work gets snagged. Typically this will be a particular person who's in high demand, but it may also be a piece of equipment that's in high demand.

If you know the bottleneck, you need to quantify the effects. There are many important issues to address. Start with these two key questions:

- How much slack does this bottleneck cause for your team in the worst case?
- What are the options for dealing with that problem?

If you're not yet sure where the bottleneck is, your situation is even more difficult.

In either case, you need to rely on your team for information

The Cost of Honesty

To better appreciate the level of risk that surrounds asking questions about workload and constraints, consider this case that we encountered. The clerical staff at a medical partnership volunteered that they weren't very busy and could find many ways to help the organization in their extra time. Their reward for volunteering was that two of them were summarily fired—and then the remaining two no longer had any extra time. Most people will feel threatened if you ask point-blank how busy they are. In many organizations, there's just no acceptable and safe answer to that question. How would the members of your team feel about these four medical clerks who admitted to being less than fully employed? Would they admire them? Would they consider them very naïve?

in evaluating the status of the team on a regular basis. You need to ask—and you need to be able to trust the answers. Unfortunately, because of the huge pressures, real and imagined, on employees to appear completely busy (so as not to risk getting laid off) and not overworked (so as not to seem incompetent to do the work), honest teamwork naturally breaks down when you try to get straight answers here.

These questions are delicate, but you need the answers to do your job. If you already have mechanisms in place to track the status of projects (such as we'll recommend in upcoming chapters, especially in Chapter 11), your need for these interviews may be limited, but they're still a good idea on occasion.

Before You Begin

Decide what questions you want each member of your staff to answer. We make several suggestions below. Try to make this list as complete as possible, so you don't leave out any important questions, because this process will be time-consuming and you don't want to have to go through it more than once. So, prepare thoroughly.

Set an appointment with each staff member. Probably an hour is suitable.

You may want to do a test run by yourself. Ask each ques-

> ## Take the Time to Do It Right
> **TRICKS OF THE TRADE**
>
> We suggest you schedule at least an hour for each interview. That may seem like a lot, but the key to getting information is to allow enough time for a good face-to-face. To ask a score of questions and get substantive answers takes time—if you want to do it right.
>
> If you anticipate that some individuals will be more articulate or informative, it would be smart to allow them more time. Schedule their interviews before the lunch hour or at the end of the day, so you can extend the interview if you want to. When the interview is going well and you're getting a lot of information, you certainly don't want the clock to end it.

tion out loud, then allow what seems to be sufficient time for the employee to think and then to answer that question. Track the time generously; most people actually take longer than we would imagine. You may also need time for an occasional follow-up question, for clarification.

Naturally, the actual length of the interviews will vary, depending on the individual. (When it comes to interviews, employees are certainly not fungible!) It's ideal to arrange the interview schedule to allow your more articulate and informative staff members to go on at greater length.

Explain that you have two purposes in this interview. First, you're trying to find a way around immediate difficulties. Second, you're trying to improve the workflow so that matters proceed more smoothly in the future. Make sure that all members of the group understand that you're seeking input. Also, understand and make sure they understand that this is not an occasion for examining particular projects or problems. Rather, you're working on the big picture of how the various commitments of the team fit together.

In a way, you're trying to increase your power as a manager by obtaining better information and making more effective assignments. The most important thing to convey to your staff is that this is not a zero-sum game. If they perceive the power you gain to be equivalent to power that they're losing, the process will meet with stiff resistance. You need to make the

⚠️ **CAUTION!**

What's in It for Them?

If your employees feel that you're gaining power at their expense, your best attempts at interviewing them will meet resistance. As a precaution, introduce the benefits you anticipate from the process—for each of them as well as for you and for the process. Emphasize that your goal is empowerment, not increased control.

case that when they help you better understand the big picture, they're helping you be in a better position to give them the control over their own work that they prefer while delivering on the commitments of the team. If a team member helps to empower you as a manager, you need to reciprocate by empowering that person in return.

Questions to Ask

Prepare for each interview by reviewing that individual's role on the team, as you understand it. If there's a formal job description, review it as well—but only after you've tried to describe the job from what you know. (If there's a significant difference between your understanding and the job description, that may indicate a problem.) As you proceed with the interview, compare the job as you understand it with how the staff member is describing it. (Here again, if there's a significant difference between your understanding and the employee's description, that may indicate a problem.)

Here are some basic questions to ask. Feel free to add to this list in advance or to ad-lib during the interview if it appears useful to do so, but try to get answers to a core group of questions from everyone on your staff.

- What are the main parts of your work?
- What proportion of your time typically goes to each part of your work?
- What interrupts your work most frequently?
- How much time do you lose when you get interrupted?
- Can you think of ways to cut down on interruptions?
- Does last-minute work divert you from your plans?

- What sorts of last-minute work come up?
- Can you think of ways to reduce last-minute work?
- What projects do you have going now? How long will each take?
- What part of your work are you best at?
- What part of your work do you enjoy most?
- What part of your work do you wish you could get someone else to do?
- What other work around here would you be able to do?
- What other work around here would you like to learn?
- Have you had a similar job elsewhere? How were things different there?
- Can you suggest ways that we might support you better?
- Can you suggest ways that the team as a whole could be more productive?
- Are there jobs the team is doing that we should outsource?
- Are there jobs the team is not doing that we could reasonably add?
- What motivates you?
- What discourages you?

Note that your immediate goal, which is an inventory of current projects, is sandwiched in the middle of this list and not given great prominence. Note also that the questions are phrased so as to show concern for the desires and professional growth of the team member.

It's especially good if your expression of concern is honest. A good manager honestly has the best interests of the staff as a prime motivator. If you can be seen as a mentor in this situation, that's for the best, but do everything possible to be seen as an ally—and do everything possible to actually be one.

Start by Selling the Process

Most employees don't fully understand what it means to be a manager. If you're new to the role, you may not fully understand it yourself. Until a person has managed for a while, he or she

Ask Further Afield

Smart Managing   Current staff members are not the only ones with worth-while knowledge about your operation. Try to find other people who might have useful information to offer. Your supervisor and your peers may be very helpful.

The most helpful informant, where it's practical, is your predeces-sor. Even if you're trying to recover from errors made by your prede-cessor, any information that person might be willing to share may shed light on how the current situation arose and what problems that per-son resolved that you might want to be on guard against as you imple-ment changes.

will not have a gut feeling for the experience. You can't expect employees inexperienced with managing to empathize with you too much. After all, you have more authority in the situation. Asking a subordinate for sympathy is almost guaranteed to damage your working relationship with that person.

On the other hand, an employee can develop an intellectual understanding of your position and what you're trying to do. You could begin by explaining how balancing the workload among the team members is a critical part of your work. Go on to explain that, in the end, each individual's job depends on the performance of the entire team, not just on his or her own pro-ductivity. The team, in turn, depends on someone balancing the work so that the team can do it most effectively. Then, note that this job has been assigned to you and that, to do it well, you need the best possible information.

Now, in best marketer's fashion, you can exult, "But wait! There's more!"

You may have made the case for supporting the team, which may be enough to motivate some people, but deep down inside everyone there's a little voice asking, "But what's in it for me?" It's best if you can get the selfish tendencies and the altruistic tendencies of your staff members pulling in the same direction.

To do this, explain that one of your purposes for getting a better idea of what and how everyone is doing is to help people get the most out of their work experience that is consistent with

---

Ask for Conceptual Understanding, but Not Emotional Support

In general, it can help you do your job if the members of your team understand your role as manager, at least to some extent. Occasionally mention how your work is intended to maximize the delivery of the entire team, rather than that of any individual, and how someone needs to keep the big picture in mind. If anyone expresses curiosity, explain as much of your job as is of interest to that person and doesn't violate any confidentiality constraints.

On the other hand, avoid asking subordinates for emotional understanding. Refrain from sharing your emotions, particularly negative emotions, with your staff. They may tend to exaggerate the import of you having a bad day. Always be cool and somewhat reserved around your staff. Don't even let go at the holiday office party.

Smart Managing

---

the goals of the larger organization. Explain that you'll be asking about likes and dislikes, strengths and weaknesses, so you can find the most effective way to support each individual in achieving personal goals within the organization.

Don't say, "I'm not here to threaten you," for the same reason that President Nixon should never have said, "I am not a crook." You don't want any of your team members even considering the possibility.

Proceed Carefully

CAUTION!

Most workers feel enormous pressure to claim that they're neither overloaded nor underloaded, so getting the information you need may not be easy. You may need to probe with questions about interruptions and concerns, for example, to get them to open up. Again, the process may take a little time, so don't rush it.

Listen and Empathize

This is a good occasion to brush up on interviewing skills. We'll cover the essentials here. A good place to learn more is the book *Smart Questions: The Essential Strategy for Successful Managers* (New York: Berkley Books, 1987) by Dorothy Leeds.

The single most important piece of interviewing advice is to ask open-ended questions. That is, avoid asking questions that will likely elicit one-word answers. Rather, aim for questions that provoke thought and reflection from your employee.

Your job in an interview is to listen and to elicit information. You're not there to share information or feelings or tell jokes or brag. You're encouraging another human to talk about matters in a situation where he or she may, realistically or not, feel at risk. (It doesn't matter how secure you feel the employee's position to be. You will feel that it's safer than your own, but he or she won't necessarily share your feelings.) Some people may feel more comfortable than others. In any case, you'll get the best information if you make each person as relaxed as possible.

Now that you've made the case for cooperation, it may help to begin with an honest compliment. After that, limit what you say or do to expressing interest and support for that person's hopes and showing concern for his or her fears.

Make eye contact to the extent that the other person will allow it. Nod to indicate comprehension. Speak in mild tones. Listen carefully—and don't jump in with the next question. Move from question to question as smoothly as possible; asking your questions as if you were reading from a script may cause your employees to limit their answers.

If an employee expresses an interesting thought, say nothing for as long as is socially comfortable, allowing the person time to volunteer an elaboration. If the silence lasts a bit too long, say

Taking Notes

TOOLS   Key tools in an interview situation are a pen and a pad of paper. You'll need to take good notes. The interview process is wasted if you can't remember what was said. Also, when you take notes, you send the message that you're taking seriously what the employee is telling you.

You might be tempted to record the conversation, to save yourself the effort of taking notes, but we recommend against tape recorders in this instance. The presence of a tape recorder can make an already uncomfortable situation worse. Besides, if you think that spending an hour to interview each employee is a lot of time to invest, do you really want to spend another hour to listen to each tape? And, even if so, you'll still want to make at least a few notes from the tapes.

something like "That's interesting. Could you elaborate?" or "Tell me more."

Rephrase what the employee says when you can, especially if you're not sure you understand. Say something like "So you don't like doing the paste-up work, then?" Don't repeat everything, though; it wastes time and shifts the focus somewhat away from the employee.

Although your immedi-

> ### The Power of Silence
> In the interview, listen attentively and respond to show understanding. Use as few words as possible. Keep to yourself any ideas that arise during the interview. For the moment, your job is to focus on hearing what each employee has to say. Experienced interviewers learn to let pauses grow long—often the most interesting comments come next.
>
> Don't worry about how you feel about the pauses; be sensitive to how the employee feels. That's what matters here.

ate short-run goal for the interview is to get time estimates for tasks, don't stress that point. Many employees are very reluctant to make estimates of how long a task will take and many are surprisingly poor at making such estimates. Keep those facts in mind as you get estimates. Emphasize that you're interested in estimates merely to get a clear idea of what that person is working on at present.

Don't use the word "why." It seems to cause most people to become defensive, to feel a need to justify. It's often easy to paraphrase a "why" question with a "how," as in "How does the paste-up job bother you?" rather than "Why don't you want to do paste-up?"

Also avoid "who" questions. Much as you would like to come out and ask, "Who do you suppose is the bottleneck around here?" don't do it. The employee may immediately perceive this to be an exercise in casting blame (even though you know that bottleneck is an esteemed position!) and will become cautious, guarded, and even suspicious.

Above all, act in good faith. In this interview, you're asking for the employee's trust. Deserve it. When you ask for trust, there's no sensible alternative to being trustworthy.

> ## Avoid Criticisms During the Interview
> A manager should never blurt criticisms. Any critical comments toward subordinates should always be delivered with considerable care and planning, lest negative emotions like shame or resentment be unleashed, which would make it harder to deal with the problems.
>
> An informational interview is the worst occasion for blurting criticisms. This amounts to punishing the employee for being honest and open and it encourages him or her to be as cagey as possible, not only for the rest of the interview, but in general. This can cause long-term damage to your ability to gain information to manage effectively.

Verify Your Estimates

Remember that the time estimates you receive from your staff come from unreliable sources. People almost universally underestimate how long their work will take. The more complex the work, the more unreliable the estimates. This isn't a matter of difficulty so much as a failure to remember. When estimating time for more complicated processes, it's easy to mentally skip some steps.

It's also true that some people are more unrealistic than others. In some organizations, a discount factor seems to emerge for each staff member, as in "Oh, Scott always underestimates how long something will take, so we always triple his estimates for planning." This person has a time discount factor of three!

If you're unfamiliar with the estimation skills of your team, there are three ways to check on their estimates.

The first is to look at historical evidence. There may be records of how your team has performed. You can compare how various team members performed on similar jobs in the past and evaluate their estimates accordingly.

Second, as part of your interview process you can ask various people how long it would take them to accomplish a particular task that you have not yet assigned. You may be able to glean information from the range of their answers, particularly about how they conceptualize tasks and calculate time.

Finally, you can refer your question to an outsider. Ideally, this is a person who does similar work in a different part of the organization or in a geographically remote business that doesn't directly compete with yours. You may also be able to get estimates in the literature of your field or even from your competitors' pricing strategies.

It should be obvious by now that time estimation skills are critically important to effective front-line management, especially in high-value-added service organizations. As we build feedback loops into your system in later chapters, both you and your team members will gain ways to gradually improve your time estimation skills. This in turn will improve the effectiveness of the entire team.

The Overload Exercise with the Team

Ideally, you'll collect enough information in your interviews to start extending the work overload exercise of Chapter 5 to the entire team. Doing so in the most general case is quite difficult, because of the numerous ways that many tasks can be assigned to many people. However, the insights of this chapter should have shown you the way to a shortcut.

Only one or two members of your staff will be the critical human resource. You may also have some machine that's critical in a similar way. You will most likely need to perform the overload exercise only on each of these resources (human or inanimate) to determine if the team is overloaded.

If they're overloaded, you'll need to take corrective action as described in Chapter 6. If, on the other hand, your critical resources are not overloaded, you'll probably have no difficulty assigning projects to your staff.

There are possible complications.

Consider, for example, this situation. Bob is the critical team member. There are two jobs, both due 12 days from now, and each takes 10 days, of which Bob must do the first five. Bob has 10 days' work to do in the next 12, so he's apparently not overloaded. The rest of your staff has 10 days of work in the next 12, which should present no problem.

But, of course, there's no way to schedule this, because of the sequence of operations. Bob has to do the first five days' work on each project. That means that the staff might have seven days to complete the first project, but, since Bob cannot finish his work on the second project until day 10, the staff would have only two days to complete the second project.

This is a simple example. In real situations, much more complicated versions of the same problem can arise. There are two ways to proceed.

You could take the time and trouble to maintain a formal software project management system. Whether this is a good idea depends primarily on the size of your projects. If most of your projects take months or years, software support is essential. If most or all of your projects take hours or days, the overhead of learning and maintaining such a system may eclipse its advantages.

In that case, you would revert to our suggestion of actually scheduling the critical resource first. While you see that Bob has only 10 days of work to complete in the next 12, you also see that he cannot complete his part of both projects before day 10, which does not allow the others to complete the second project.

Notice that while the methods of Chapter 5 are sufficient to plan the time for an individual acting alone, they may be merely indicative in team situations, because of the interrelationships of team members working on a project. To continue with our simple example, if Bob had 15 days of work to do in the next 12, you would know that there's a problem, but knowing that he has only 10 days of work to do in the next 12 is not enough to prove that there *isn't* a problem.

In the next chapter we'll discuss allocation of resources, human and otherwise. For now, focus on taking your group's pulse. Use your interviews to gain time estimates and milestones for each of the group's commitments and a clear sense of who's working on what.

Some Other Ways to Know You're in Trouble

Because your preliminary estimates based on staff input are so problematic, it pays to look for other early warning signs of pending problems.

Morale

The main one, of course, is morale. It's usually easy to distinguish a workgroup that's having a reasonable amount of fun from one that's gloomy and stressed or another that's giddy and irresponsible.

There are cultural differences, of course. Jocular teasing and wordplay are much more common in urban cultures, as are casual expressions of frustration and dismay. If you're from a more urban culture than the members of your team, you may find them excessively reserved, while if you're from a more rural culture, you may find your coworkers brazen and abrasive. After you adjust for these differences, though, you'll be able to pick up on the shifts in the state of the team's emotions.

Critical signs of bad morale:

- "That's not my job."
- "I'm doing the best I can."
- "Somebody should do that."
- "We can't afford any more mistakes."

And worst of all, of course:

- "I quit."

Fussiness About Specifications

There's a pair of indicators of trouble that in some ways are opposite. One is a complete failure to comply with formalities, which implies that an atmosphere of crisis prevails. This "too busy for procedures" attitude is toxic to the whole operation, not just the particular project at hand. The opposite indicator is a fanatical devotion to formalisms, to the extent that they interfere with productivity. This usually indicates a certain level of covering one's own behind in the expectation that bad news is immanent.

Dilbert Index

TOOLS A useful formal measure of workplace morale is what we call the Dilbert Index, which is the average number of Dilbert cartoons posted per work station. A high Dilbert Index is a good sign.

While often spectacularly funny, Dilbert cartoons are also sometimes a bit sarcastic and abrasive. A workplace that can handle the sort of mockery dished out in this cartoon and similar ones is one where morale is high. As the manager, you may be the overt or subtle target of such humor. If this happens, don't respond in any way. Of course, when humor is targeted at gender or ethnicity, this is a serious threat to a business atmosphere, but humor targeted at authority should be taken with good grace.

Delay by Redefinition

Some projects seem to grow without bound or their goals constantly shift. That may not be entirely the responsibility of the customer. Teams that are behind on a project welcome changes in specifications, because that provides cover for late delivery of milestones. In any case, even if the blame falls entirely on the customer or outside constituency, projects whose definitions keep changing are in some sort of trouble.

If any of these early warning signs are present in your work group, you have some tough times ahead. Pay careful attention to building trust and mutual understanding as you begin your interview process. As you demonstrate sincerely that you're acting in good faith, your subordinates will likely reciprocate.

Focus on the purpose of the interview process—to help you as a manager find ways around immediate difficulties and to design systems that support smooth workflow in the future.

Manager's Checklist for Chapter 8

❏ While keeping your entire team working on productive activities at 100% of capacity is the ideal, for most groups this ideal is unattainable, because incoming work can't be expected to match resources exactly.

❏ Most groups that are in a time crisis regarding pending

deliveries are limited by the performance of one or a few individuals. You can survive the crunch by identifying the critical people and focusing on offloading their tasks that can be delegated and supporting those that cannot.

❏ Consider a series of interviews with the staff, as well as with anyone else who may have useful information about your workplace. Prepare staff for the interview by showing them the advantages of an informed manager. Focus on mutual empowerment and avoid zero-sum rhetoric.

❏ Use whatever information you can to validate the staff input, particularly regarding time commitments.

❏ If you identify any time crunch, use the methods of Chapter 6 to recover.

"Second Things Never ...": The Trouble with Priorities

Princess Fiona (as she and Shrek the ogre, her rescuer, are fleeing the ferocious dragon): "You mean you didn't slay the dragon?!?"
Shrek the ogre: "It's on my to-do list!"
—from the movie *Shrek*

One motivation for this book is reliability. Our objective is to put together the knowledge, skills, and strategies for a reliable workgroup. Reliability is a win for everyone—you, your bosses, your staff, and your clients. Only your direct competitors stand to lose ground if you develop a more reliable workplace.

The fundamental components of a reliable work strategy are:

- **Knowing:** having a clear set of commitments.
- **Limiting:** accepting only those commitments that can realistically be fulfilled.
- **Planning:** allocating efforts to your commitments.

- **Tracking:** knowing the status of progress on each of your projects.
- **Controlling:** making sure projects stay on track.
- **Correcting:** repairing individual problems and tuning the system.

In this chapter, we take on the problem of making sure that your commitments are clear and realistic.

In order to be seen as responsible, you must have the same concept of your responsibilities as the people who need the end product of your work. If people think you've agreed to something that you have forgotten or weren't even aware of, you'll be seen as irresponsible. If you deliver something that no one expects or wants, you're wasting your efforts.

In order to be reliable, you also need to make sure you don't regularly bite off more than you can chew. Although a time crisis can occasionally arise from unforeseen circumstances and bad breaks, much more typically it arises from making an unrealistic set of commitments.

Often, this sort of overcommitment arises from a misunderstanding of when and how to prioritize your objectives. This misunderstanding may have its roots in a common misunderstanding of how time management systems should work.

How Commitments Get Made

A universal hallmark of a reliable individual, as of a reliable group, is a clear distinction between commitments and mere ideas. It often happens that misunderstandings occur because of personal cultural differences. Just as some people say, "I don't mind" to express enthusiasm and others use the same words to express indifference, some workers who say, "Yes, you could have it in two weeks" are expressing a commitment while others are simply expressing potential availability.

In a restaurant, the moment you place your order is usually very clear. If you find yourself in a situation of ambiguity, be sure to continue the communication until you are certain there's mutual agreement.

Often, requests are not phrased as optional. The restaurant customer who asks, "Could I have a cheeseburger?" (assuming that cheeseburgers are on the menu) is not typically listening for the answer (even though it could be negative, if the restaurant is out of burgers, buns, or cheese). "Could I have a cheeseburger?" is essentially a rhetorical question: you're not expecting an answer, just a cheeseburger.

If you're in a service business, or in a service relationship with others inside or outside your institution, you may not always have the option of refusing a request. In other situations, contracting and consulting businesses, for example, the workload is directly negotiable. In such situations, it's especially critical that you, as a manager, have a clear idea of the workload. This isn't always easy.

The first problem is that the system does not distinguish between *projects* and *tasks*. Here, we use our definition for tasks from Chapter 4: a unit of work that can in principle be undertaken by a single person without interruption, therefore in less than a single workday. Clearly, if items are to go from the master list directly to the calendar, only tasks that can be done in a day will ever make the transition.

This problem is easily handled. For example, as a master list item, instead of putting "build bridge," put "plan first phase

"I'm Fine with Doing That"

Is that an agreement or just an agreement in principle?

A production manager for a graphic design studio had been closely managing one new employee, giving specific assignments, while managing the interactions with the customer herself. Feeling that he was ready for more responsibility, she sat down with him and said that he was now ready to manage the customer communications and deliveries directly. He agreed, amicably, saying, "I'm fine with that." Some weeks later, the customer called her to complain about very bad service. She sought out her employee and reminded him of their earlier conversation. He nodded, saying, "I'm fine with that. When is that going to start?"

of building bridge." Planning can generate multiple tasks, which you can then schedule as appropriate.

A related problem is the visibility of the deadline. To-do items that represent multiple tasks are often started too late, because the required start date is not obvious. The to-do method doesn't handle threads well. A solution is to break the thread into tasks and list all of them.

The To-Do-List Trap

Most time management strategies miss this point. We've seen the error carried over to group management errors as well. The problem generally shows up as a misplaced and inappropriate emphasis on prioritization.

Consider how priority appears in standard time management strategies. The usual suggestion is that a person should have a master to-do list, containing everything that needs to be done. As an item comes to mind, the person adds it to the master list and assigns a priority, usually on a scale of one to three, five, or 10. (Sometimes the three levels are designated as the "A list," the "B list, " and the "C list," in decreasing order of priority.)

Then, during weekly or daily planning, the person moves items from the master list onto the calendar. Generally, if there are any A list items, these are moved onto the calendar first.

Some systems make this easier by encouraging users to parcel out their time into roles. This can substitute a half-dozen shorter master lists for a single long one, which can be very helpful in maintaining a balanced life. Some fundamental problems remain, though.

It's remarkable how well this system works for some people—and how badly it works for others. Many people castigate themselves for failing to maintain this system, when in fact the problem is that the system is simply not equipped to handle the sorts of work that they do.

The fundamental problem is that the commitment process is muddled and there's no check for feasibility. Whenever anything "to do" comes up, it's added to the "to-do" list. The only real commitment occurs when an item is moved from the list to the calendar.

Making an item a high priority may help, but it's no guarantee the item will get done. If a person generates high-priority to-do list items more rapidly than he or she completes those items, then the list will continually grow. This means that more and more tasks remain undone.

Adding due dates may help, especially for a person with flexible work hours, but even so, there's nothing in this mechanism to prevent overcommitment.

Many busy people dutifully create to-do lists with lower-priority items as well, even though they never get caught up on their A list. The B list grows even faster than the A list, since very few items are ever removed from it! The C list, if it exists, simply becomes a depository for an odd sort of fiction.

The more creative and the more ambitious or well-meaning the person, the longer and more unwieldy his or her to-do lists become and the more difficult it is to identify items from the to-do list that are candidates for the current week's calendar. Eventually, items that have a due date associated with them don't find a place on the calendar and are dropped.

The underlying problem is easy to understand. This sort of to-do list is open-ended. There's no way to tell from the to-do list whether you're overcommitted or not. There's nothing constraining you from adding items to the to-do list, even though your time is limited. This method may have little negative consequence when used for handling discretionary items, such as "Give Mary more public acknowledgment for writing reports," but it's a poor method for managing commitments, such as "Deliver report to customer." Adding a to-do, even with a due date and a high priority, does not guarantee that the item can feasibly be done.

Time-Budgeted To-Do's (Commitments) vs. Optional To-Do's (Ideas)

The to-do method can be modified to distinguish between an item that is a good idea to do and an item for which time has been budgeted. If you maintain your time-crunch analysis on a regular basis, you can have a clear idea when you can add items to your list of actual commitments.

In other words, it's possible to maintain two master lists: one for things that would be good to do and the other for commitments, that is, items that are not yet on your calendar but are already accounted for in your time budget (Figure 9-1).

Master List	Commitment List			
To do eventually	Commitment	Effort (hrs)	Due	Sched.
Get web contractor	Replace locks and keys	6	12/2	❏
New logo and campaign	Christmas mailing	4	12/5	❏
Purge files	Plan Chicago trip	2	12/3	❏
Call, close old prospects	Chicago trip	28	12/15	❏
Review error process				
Rearrange library				
Plan Chicago trip				
Plan Minneapolis trip				
Buy new gizmotron				
Review Jones project				
Smith proposal				

Figure 9-1. Master list and commitment list
Many people put tasks and projects as they think of them on a master to-do list, but do not budget time for the tasks. This works if a person is not too busy. This example shows a modified to-do list, which contains a master list and a much shorter commitment list. Items are only moved to the commitment list when time is budgeted for them. This still allows a place to keep every idea and inspiration, but is scheduled effectively. The example here shows the list just when a Chicago trip is put into the time budget.

> ### Sort Your to-Do List
>
> **Smart Managing** Distinguish between ideas and commitments. It's often said that a plan is an idea with a due date, but a commitment is more than that. A commitment is a plan that you can be confident that you'll fulfill. A commitment is a plan for which time is budgeted.
>
> One way to handle this is never to commit to anything without scheduling it immediately. Another is to maintain a time budget and two to-do lists, one for commitments that have had an impact on your time budget, though they may not be scheduled yet, another for ideas—options, theories, maybes, and "when-I-get-around-to-it's."
>
> You'll periodically need to purge your idea list of outdated and unrealistic items. Otherwise, it'll grow too unwieldy to be of use.

A somewhat simpler, if more constraining approach is never to commit to anything without immediately scheduling it. In that approach, your to-do list can contain only ideas and no commitments at all.

Without some sort of constraint from your time budget, your to-do list will grow endlessly—and the sense you will have and will convey to others is that you do not fulfill your commitments.

The Productivity Paradox

In the typical workplace, work is a marathon, not a sprint. Successful long-distance runners don't expend the maximum available effort at all moments. They understand that to do so would deplete their energy too soon and hurt their performance in the long run.

Rather than working toward maximum effort, the winner aims for maximum *sustainable* effort. The winner of the race paces performance so as to maintain reserves of energy for the long run. Similarly, a well-designed workplace works toward maximum sustainable productivity.

Unfortunately, many workplaces demand maximum effort from everyone at all times, as if work were a sprint. This is like imagining a 50-kilometer race as a 100-meter sprint run 500 times in a row. A runner who takes on a marathon in that way will start out ahead, but will fall behind the pack before too long.

Maximum sustainable productivity Top productivity that an individual or group can achieve over a long time. For any group of people, given their skills and other resources, there's a theoretical maximum, which is the optimum you should aim for as a manager.

The productivity of any worker depends on two factors—the level of effort and the level of efficiency, defined as production per unit of effort. In the short run, increasing effort always leads to greater production. This is like a sprint, where total production per unit of time is critical. However, in most work situations, the long-term average of productivity is more important than maximum episodic productivity.

For low-maintenance machines, these levels of productivity are identical, since machines don't get tired. People, on the other hand, decline in performance under sustained stress. Therefore, the maximum sustainable productivity is lower than maximum episodic productivity.

A very common symptom of the high-stress workplace is perpetual prioritization. Work is driven by the urgency *du jour*, rather than by a well-thought out plan that links short-term activity and long-term activity. Rather than encouraging working toward long-term goals, such a workplace actively derides these efforts. The motto of the stress-driven workplace is "We don't have time for that now."

The immediate result of this constant urgency, of course, is systematically reduced productivity of the same sort as affects the marathon runner who runs the race as if it were a sprint. Forgive us for repeating ourselves, but this is important.

The team that is always putting maximum effort toward immediate goals will not generally perform as well as the team that performs at a slightly lower level of effort, because the lower level is more efficient over the long run.

Prioritization as a Symptom

Another consequence of always running at full tilt toward the next immediate objective is that subsequent objectives are set aside since "that's not a priority right now." Then, they disappear from sight and may die a quiet death—or they may fester until they "suddenly" erupt, to become the next crisis for the unwary high-stress workgroup.

Among those objectives are items that you may have happily agreed to do, but that never rose to the level of highest priority. Perhaps you never specified a clear delivery date. Perhaps you did, but neglected it in the face of a "more important" project that attained crisis proportions around the same time.

Most insidiously, perhaps the commitment was internal, made to a staff member. In a real crisis it may be necessary to defer internal commitments; staff members may be understanding about such delays. However, a permanent state of crisis effectively prevents managers from ever addressing internal commitments. The result?

- Any promises you make to your staff in the future are less credible.
- You weaken your authority to hold others to their commitments.
- You permanently damage morale within the team.

Commitments abandoned or forgotten in the blur of perpetual crisis are the essence of unreliability.

We consulted with one chronically overcommitted group that explicitly used red or green folders to contain documents related to high- or low-priority items. The result, of course, was that they never got around to the green folders.

Some items had been put into the green folders because when they arrived their deadlines were far off enough that they could be addressed easily. Since they stayed in green folders, however, they became invisible until it was almost too late (at which time they were promoted to red folders) or definitely too late (at which time they became public embarrassments).

The solution that we recommended to this group was simple. We advised them to stop using the green folders. You may object (as they did, quite vehemently) that they were already busy enough with their existing load. This is precisely true, but it's precisely the problem.

Priority Problems

In a local publishing company, the manager of the graphics department wanted to control the flow of incoming projects. She established a system of allowing her internal customers to label their orders as high priority by affixing a red label.

The result? As you might have guessed, the little red stickers began to proliferate. Employees who had less urgent projects were unwilling to take the chance that fellow employees would fill the schedule with a queue of projects labeled high-priority. What began as an effort to control the flow failed to do so—and caused competition and conflicts among coworkers.

If your solution is to make some commitments less important than others, that's the opposite of a solution. It absolutely guarantees that many commitments will be neglected. The only real solution is better gatekeeping—better control over the incoming workload.

Prioritization and Gatekeeping

The crisis-driven group is making the same mistake as the crisis-driven individual who has no gatekeeping on his or her to-do list. We recommend that each individual regularly take inventory of the total time already committed on the personal to-do list, using the workload calculation method described in Chapter 5, and refrain from taking on work that's unrealistic. In the same way, the manager of a workgroup must always know whether the group is committed close to its capacity and, if so, be very careful about taking on additional commitments.

How does your group maintain its to-do list? For most groups, the to-do list is a figure of speech. Nevertheless, your team takes on commitments in some way.

Before you began interviewing your team members, you may not have had a systematic way of knowing what your group was committed to. Perhaps you had a way to view most of your obligations, but not all of them. When you complete the interviews described in Chapter 8, you have a worthwhile snapshot of your team's current commitments.

The Best Way to Reduce Workload

Smart Managing   The workgroup that's fully committed is in its ideal—but fragile—optimum state. Such a workgroup needs to be careful about taking on too much additional work.

Workgroups that do private sector work for outside customers are in an ideal position to manage workload. They simply need to raise their rates to the point where demand is slightly below their capacity. This not only makes for a less stressful workplace, it also increases profits!

Many small businesses resist this step. "I wouldn't pay that much for those services," they say. Of course you wouldn't. You're the expert at this work. Why would you pay someone else? If your time isn't more valuable to others than it is to you, you wouldn't have a business at all. Being too busy is a sign that you're doing well. So, why not turn a minus into a plus?

Note that the raise-the-rates strategy does not have an effect on work commitments already in house; for the short term you'll probably need another strategy.

Look over the list of current commitments and consider how they were agreed to. Which are part of the central ongoing responsibilities of your workgroup and which are projects? Which are agreed to on an ongoing basis? Which might realistically be done by vendors, clients, or third parties?

You can categorize your commitments as follows:

- Ongoing and necessary
- Ongoing but potentially outsourced
- On demand
- On demand but potentially outsourced
- On demand but potentially discouraged or refused or delayed

To maximize production, you need to approach your sustainable level without risking greatly exceeding it. Clearly, as your group approaches the status of being fully committed, you need to invoke an option to refuse or discourage or outsource additional work.

To do this, in turn, you need to know current status on an

ongoing basis, an issue that we'll discuss in Chapter 11. If there's no possibility of outsourcing, discouraging, deferring, or refusing tasks, you're in a very difficult position. From a systems engineering point of view, you are running open-loop, with nothing preventing outside influences from making too many demands on you. We've seen public sector services in this unfortunate situation; the only advice we can offer is for them to look for ways to cut corners and do a less adequate job. (This can have tragic consequences in the society at large, but the workers in these situations have no choice but to do the best they can with the resources available.)

Prioritization and Goal-Setting

The essence of reliability is to distinguish as little as possible among commitments. A commitment is a commitment. Once a commitment is made, there should be no prioritization.

What, then, of setting goals, of being the master of your own fate? We're not denying you that authority and responsibility. In fact, the goals and priorities that you set for yourself and your team are critical to the gatekeeping function. But the time to set priorities is *before* you make commitments, not *after*.

For instance, your goal may be to move toward more profitable types of jobs. You may bid for a lower profit margin on a type of work that you would like to get into. You may bid at a higher profit on work that you are currently doing but would like to avoid in the future. For example, a print shop may set a higher priority on getting glossy magazines than on getting newsletters.

All of these calculations, however, must precede the acceptance of a job. After a job is accepted, a well-functioning team will deliver it on time and to spec, whether or not the work fits the team's longer-term goals and directions. That's no longer an issue after you've made the commitment. If our print shop doesn't produce the newsletter it's agreed to produce, it will be perceived as unreliable, and its chance of getting contracts for glossy magazines will decline.

It's central to your work as manager to ensure that, in pursuing its goals, your group is as highly committed as is sustainable, but not more so. There is a risk-benefit tradeoff regarding how close to that line you want to get, but consistently staying at an unsustainable workload is foolish and futile.

How you achieve your maximum sustainable productivity depends a lot on your situation. Go over all the commitments that emerged in your conversations with the team and understand exactly how and when these commitments were made. If necessary, place limitations on who's empowered to commit the group to some activities. If possible, set appropriate conditions on which work is accepted and which is not. If you're dealing with a few large projects, it may be feasible for you to act as gatekeeper yourself. If your business deals with a very large number of smaller projects, you will need to set policies or prices to control the workload. Each specific situation will require an appropriate strategy in response.

The goals of your gatekeeping are simply stated, if not necessarily easy to achieve:

- Know how busy you are and when.
- Know and control how and when new commitments are made.
- Encourage extra work when idle and discourage it when busy.

The details of how you achieve these goals are up to you.

Prioritization in Crisis

Of course, if your building is on fire, save lives first, then worry about saving your business later. In other words, priorities can still matter in action as well as in planning.

We did use prioritization methods in our chapters on escaping from crisis. What's more, because the productive team operates close to capacity in an uncertain world, crises will occasionally arise. At those times, it's essential to look over your commitments and reallocate your attentions to maximum utility.

The Curse of the Double Victory

Two wrongs don't make a right, but two rights can make a wrong!

During the recent technology boom, opportunities abounded for programming shops. We know of a group that pursued two contracts, each of which would be very lucrative but very demanding.

Times being what they were, the group landed both jobs at about the same time. The group was unable to find additional qualified workers, so it was desperately overcommitted. Unfortunately, they lacked a mechanism for short-circuiting an active bid once their calendar was full. In the end, they barely managed the delivery, but not without losing a key staff member due to the demands and stress of meeting these two contracts simultaneously. The products were marginal and they failed to hold onto either customer after the first delivery.

Our point in this chapter is not that you shouldn't prioritize in crisis. It's that you shouldn't be in perpetual crisis. If you're always using the methods of prioritization to decide what to do next, you need to reconsider how your operation is working.

Under ordinary circumstances, treat every commitment as a top priority. An effective organization rarely has to reprioritize.

Manager's Checklist for Chapter 9

❏ Conventional time management muddles the moment of commitment with to-do lists. It is difficult to know when a to-do list is overloaded. One can maintain an ongoing workload estimate, or can directly schedule new work. Otherwise there is constant risk of overcommitment.

❏ Workgroups often lack even the equivalent of a to-do list. There is a need for a formal inventory of all commitments of the group, and an ongoing estimate of workload.

❏ Teams that are constantly prioritizing work are in constant crisis, and are therefore working below capacity and above the needed level of stress.

❏ Prioritization is very important in crisis recovery, and in goal setting and planning, but ongoing, chronic prioritization of active tasks is symptomatic of systematic problems.

❏ The place to control the workload is at the time and place that commitments are made, not afterward.

❏ In normal conditions, all agreed–upon commitments have the same priority. This should be changed only in a rare crisis situation.

Allocation for Efficiency:
The Importance of Compartmentalization

In the previous chapter, we emphasized how critical it is to control your workload at the source. It's impossible to perform reliably if you have too many commitments. In the face of a natural tendency to accept all opportunities and the inherent difficulties in estimating workload, controlling workload isn't always easy, though the workload estimation strategy we described in Chapter 5 can be very helpful.

Of course, we aren't done yet. It isn't enough that we now have strategies in place so that reliability is feasible. Ensuring that it's possible to direct attention to the right project at the right time is only the first step. Now we have to make sure it actually happens.

In personal time management, this is the step in which items move from the to-do list to the calendar. In managing the attentions of the group, you have the same problems multiplied. If there are nine people on your team, the problem is at least multiplied ninefold. In fact, in most workgroups it's even more challenging than that. The team members have overlapping skills and mutually contingent responsibilities. What each person is doing at any moment depends to a great extent on the success or failure of other team members.

Personal time management, done right, takes about an hour a week. Managing the time of nine people and the equipment they share can be the main component of a full-time job. It may well be the main component of yours.

A reliable organization fulfills almost every commitment it makes, delivering timely warnings and appropriate compensation on the few exceptions. Nothing is forgotten, dropped, or left hanging indefinitely. Maintaining reliability in the face of this complexity is a simply stated goal, but one that's not easy to achieve. There is no one-size-fits-all strategy for reliability.

The Airtight System

There are some universal principles that apply, though. The essence of an airtight system is to ensure that effort is expended on every commitment in a timely fashion. Nothing can be forgotten or abandoned.

In the last chapter, we explained how effective gatekeeping at the input of the system was the first step. It's only the first step. Effective gatekeeping ensures that a path to your goals exists. You still need to plan that path.

The Efficiency Paradox

For most aspects of management, the better your team is working, the less work you need to do. The fewer the conflicts or morale issues, the less you need to intervene. The more the staff understands and agrees with your mission and strategy, the less leadership effort you need to expend. The better your integration with the larger organization, the less you'll need to exert your influence in internal negotiations.

Allocation of efforts is fundamentally different from other aspects of management. The better your team is performing, the more work you'll have to do. The better you perform your allocated duties, the more your team can accomplish. The pay-off is a high-performance team, but the cost is an increasing effort to manage its daily efforts. It takes more skill and attention to drive a racecar at top speed than to commute to work at the posted speed limit. That's the efficiency paradox.

For example, one way the team can be more efficient is to increase the overlap between the skill sets of the people on the staff. If only one person knows how to run a particular process, some of your projects may be on hold if that person is ill or has other responsibilities. If you have another person who can do that work, your projects are much less likely to be delayed. Your team is better off. On the other hand, every time that task comes up in the future, you'll have to decide which person to assign it to. One cost of the increased capacity of the team is that you have an extra decision to make.

Many aspects of management are about avoiding problems or, in other words, about reducing costs. Effective planning is about delivering. Effective control of time and deliveries is where you as a manager have the opportunity to add positive value to your organization. To make the most of this opportunity, you need to be smart, sensitive, and diligent.

Project Evaluation and Review Technique (PERT)

Large-scale, high-stakes design-and-build projects involving multiple threads are generally managed using PERT or the critical path method or its derivatives. Usually, a project management software package is used to plan and allocate effort in this environment.

The principles involved in this sort of project management are worth knowing, even if they do not apply directly to your circumstances. You can find a succinct and clear formal introduction in Chapter 12 of *Operations Management* by Jae K. Shim and Joel G. Siegel (New York: Barron's Educational Series, 1999). There's a more leisurely presentation in *Project Management* by Gary R. Heerkens (New York: McGraw-Hill, 2002).

> **Project Evaluation and Review Technique (PERT)** A methodology for planning, scheduling, and coordinating complex projects with multiple threads. Its aim is to offer systematic plans on how to proceed, and ongoing estimates of whether a project is on schedule and on budget. Dependencies between aspects of the project are carefully mapped out and valuable resources are allocated for specific time windows. Contemporary project managers usually use complex software to support this effort.
>
> While this approach is not usually appropriate for the workplace with a larger number of simpler projects, any manager would benefit from understanding its principles.

Understanding the basics of how small numbers of large projects are handled can be helpful in identifying the issues in the multiple-project environment. On the other hand, these methods don't typically apply directly to the workplace with a large number of small projects.

Here are situations where project management software is a good idea:

- A single project or a small number of large projects
- Multiple projects of similar size and structure
- Multithreading within projects, requiring critical path analysis
- Large subtasks, with infrequent handoffs
- High predictability, limited dependence on uncontrolled events
- High stakes, justifying extensive planning per project

The more these circumstances hold, the more effective advance planning can be and the more added value can be obtained from a precise schedule set in advance.

While many of the ideas in this book will be a useful supplement to people doing this sort of project management, those managers are already well served by an extensive body of theory and practice.

There's a broad range of activities where PERT, in combination with project management software, can be very effective. However, there are two important caveats:

- Operating the software effectively is more than knowing what the menus and controls do. It requires considerable skill and careful consideration of the underlying goals of the organization and of the skills and weaknesses of the assigned staff.
- Although PERT and associated software are very useful in many circumstances and indispensable in some, there are other cases where PERT is simply inappropriate.

We're primarily concerned here with workgroups that deal with the following:

- Many projects, interspersed with ongoing routine responsibilities
- A wide variety of projects and work patterns, some very small
- Little or no multithreading—when one job is on hold, you can pick up another
- Many handoffs
- Possibly large uncertainty on duration of tasks compared to project duration
- Much skills overlap among staff
- Moderate stakes per project, limiting managerial availability per project
- Unpredictable, dependent on uncontrollable events

These circumstances make detailed advance allocation of resources more problematic and increase the likelihood that corrections to the schedule will be necessary. They also raise the proportional cost of planning relative to other work, since many of the planned steps will be short. Most important of all, they decrease the value of detailed advance planning.

As we defined it in Chapter 7, a critical path is the series of consecutive activities that represent the longest path through a multithreaded project. The critical path determines the earliest possible delivery of the entire project.

Take an auto assembly line, for instance. If the body and the engine of a car are assembled at the same time, with a final step of dropping the engine into the body, the final step is on the critical path, as is whichever assembly thread is of longer duration. If the body can be assembled more quickly than the engine, its duration is irrelevant to the total time to assemble the vehicle: it's not part of the critical path.

If there's only one thread in a project, the entire project is the critical path. Such a project will not be completed until every one of the tasks is done in sequence; its duration will be the sum of the durations of its component tasks. This is the usual case with small projects.

In a highly multithreaded project, it's more important to identify the critical path and to track the threads. The word "critical" is not used unreasonably. The availability of staff and resources for critical path work is essential, because if such work is delayed, many other scheduled and allocated resources become idle—and the impacts may cascade for years.

On the other hand, the workgroup that's dealing with a large number of independent projects is much less vulnerable to this sort of disruption. When each project is only a single thread, a step that's late may prevent others from proceeding on that

---

The Accountant's Office

An accounting firm is a good example of a multiple-project workplace. Like any other business, it's subject to delays because of changed customer specifications.

If a customer calls up during tax preparation season saying, "Wait, there's a 1099 form I forgot to send along," that one return may be delayed. This has very little impact on the accounting firm's other work. It simply frees up attention for all the other tax returns. The customer who forgot a form is at risk of having to file late, but has not damaged the progress of the firm to do useful work.

At a workplace that has many projects, the impact of an unexpected delay is small. Therefore, the advantage of detailed scheduling of individual tasks is also small. If every tax return had been entered into project management software, this delay would have meant considerable effort in updating the schedule, even though it would not prevent the work from getting done.

work. However, there are many other pieces of work for the team to do that do not depend in any way on that item. The delay of a single project, while problematic for that particular delivery, frees up resources for other work, rather than idling them.

In summary, for the workplace with many small, simple projects rather than a few large, complex ones, advance planning is more difficult and more expensive, but it's also less important. While it's worth knowing the principles of formal project management and perhaps roughing out a sketch of the upcoming work dependencies every week or so, maintaining a rigorous formal project plan in a complex software package is, in many circumstances, a waste of effort.

Compartmentalization

Formal project management and intuitive management are the extreme points of a spectrum. (Chapter 3 dealt with the topic of this spectrum in some detail.)

The intuitively managed workplace has one sort of time, "work time," and the manager and the subordinates allocate that time from day to day as needed. This risks confusion and failure.

The formal project management schedule places every single item in a precise schedule. There's a separate sort of time for each task. This risks excessive and unrealistic planning in the multiple-project workplace.

What's the alternative, then? If informal, intuitive methods are overwhelmed, but detailed planning is excessive, is there a middle ground? How do we go about ensuring that every work item gets its share of attention?

The middle ground is to categorize the types of work and ensure that every

> **Compartmentalization** *Key Term*
> The division of the efforts of an individual or a team into particular categories. This structuring of effort is a good intermediate strategy between total informality (sometimes called "seat-of-the-pants" management) and the complete formality of the PERT method.

commitment is assigned to an appropriate category. Our word for this is "compartmentalization." The idea is the simple and ancient one that there's a time for every purpose. This proverbial wisdom has sometimes been lost in the hubbub of modern life. In other words, at any time, there's one thing to pay attention to and a vast array of things to leave aside.

Dividing Attention Among Incompatible Tasks

It's interesting how some workplaces are open door and others are closed door. In some places, interruptions are welcome and there's much conversation in the hallways, around the water cooler, and in meeting rooms. In other workplaces, casual conversation is discouraged and meetings are rare and usually intended to address major issues.

As a manager, you're pulled in both directions. You need to be accessible to your customers or constituents, to your supervisors, and to your staff. If a staff member is stuck because of a decision that's outside his or her authority, it's best if you can respond promptly. If a staff member has a more serious problem, it's best for morale if you're available as soon as possible.

On the other hand, you probably have concentrated work that you need to do, involving such tasks as contracting, reporting, and planning. These tasks are difficult to do when you're frequently being interrupted.

One of the pieces of advice that we offer most frequently is for the manager to compartmentalize his or her time. Some time blocks should be designated as "open door" and others as "closed door." This is almost universal practice among college and university faculty. A professor will usually post "office hours" for the current semester on his or her office door (and now on the Web) and announce them at the beginning of the first meeting of any course. It's surprising that many managers do not have a comparable way to distinguish between interruptible and non-interruptible time.

Notice how this simple compartmentalization of time enhances both types of activity. You can carry on concentrated work without constant disruption, yet staff feel free to bring their concerns to you during particular times, increasing your contact with them and your understanding of the present status of production work.

What about occasions when you need to cancel your open-door time? You may have an urgent delivery of your own to produce or you may even be out of town. This is tolerable if it's occasional and you announce it in advance. However, if this becomes habitual, you're undermining your credibility, so be careful and take your open-door policy seriously.

While we're on the subject of your own time, it's probably worthwhile to issue a warning. Tom DeMarco calls this warning "don't put yourself in as your own utility infielder" and we call it "don't run the laminating machine in the basement," in honor of our friend Sarah White. The point is that effective management sometimes requires unstructured attention to the overall process. A manager should not, in general, allow his or her

---

Don't Run the Laminating Machine in the Basement

⚠️ **CAUTION!**

The successful manager will, after some months of solving problems, find himself or herself with some free time. This is not a problem. This is an opportunity for researching new opportunities for the organization.

The beginning manager, having recently been a production employee, and perhaps still having the worldview of the production worker, is vulnerable at this point to being accused of not working hard enough, rather than congratulated for past success. The temptation is great to move part of the manager's schedule back into production.

In one case that we know, the manager's reward for greatly improving the process at an organization was to be assigned one of its least desirable production jobs, running the laminating machine in the basement, to fill in her slack time.

Except in extreme situations, this is a mistake to be avoided. The captain should not be in the hold pulling oars with everyone else while no one is steering. A manager returning to production work may be avoiding unfamiliar responsibilities rather than helping the team as a whole.

Divide Your Time into Open Door and Closed Door

Smart Managing

Managers need to be maximally accessible to staff and outsiders. Yet managers also must focus on difficult tasks like drawing up complex plans and proposals or reviewing technical production. The former responsibility requires being open to interruptions, while the latter requires avoiding interruptions.

The best approach is to divide the hours in your week into open-door and closed-door times. If possible, aim for consistent open-door hours from week to week.

Remember that you should be dedicated to facilitating the productivity of the members of your team; they're not responsible for facilitating yours. Allow them to interrupt you, but be very careful about interrupting any of the members of your high-value production staff. It's always a good idea to send an e-mail or to at least stop by for a second to say, "Please come and talk to me when you reach a good stopping point."

slack to be taken up by relatively low-value production work. This mistake is particularly tempting when it's least appropriate, in a work crunch. It's at the time when meeting all commitments is most difficult that the manager's attention is most required in a managerial capacity. Moving the manager into production in a crunch is the opposite of helping.

This isn't to say that you can't have some background work that keeps you current on the latest techniques. Keeping up with the field is more difficult for managers than for production staff, so having a non-urgent project going in the background is a fine idea. It's not a bad idea, for example, for a laminating manager to know how to operate a laminating machine. But for the manager to pitch in for deadline-driven work is almost always a mistake.

Allocating Attention to Low-Visibility Commitments

The principle of compartmentalization can be extended to the group in two ways. One is simply to repeat what you did for yourself, by advocating that individuals divide their time into two or more compartments that support incompatible sorts of activities. Another is to divide the team as a whole into separate subgroups with different key responsibilities. This can be a way to ensure that items that otherwise might slip through the cracks get their due attention.

If we agree that all commitments, in principle, are at the same priority level, we nevertheless have some more prominently in mind than others. Compartmentalizing across the team is one way to make sure that the squeaky wheel doesn't get all the grease.

Attending to Critical Resources

Recall that the most important aspect of planning is reducing unnecessary load on critical resources. We can assist in this by dividing tasks up into categories.

For instance, suppose that Harry is your production employee in greatest demand. For any task, then, you can ask the question, "Is Harry the only person who can do this?" If so, it's a "Harry-only" category of task. If not, assign it to another employee.

You and Harry, meanwhile, should compartmentalize Harry's

The Amoeba Method

We worked with a small company that produced promotional graphics for advertising campaigns. One of its customers had been enormously successful; in fact, the scale of the work for that customer had grown to the point where the company could not survive without this big account. The company needed to develop more and better small accounts, yet the attentions of the entire staff were constantly devoted to the demands of the large customer.

The solution ("the amoeba method") was to divide the production staff into two teams of roughly similar capabilities. One team was designated the "small accounts" team: members of this team were to place the demands of smaller customers ahead of the demands of the big customer. Satisfaction with the company's performance soared among the smaller accounts. Today the largest customer generates a smaller fraction of the total revenue of the business.

By assigning a team to treat the smaller accounts as a top priority, the small company overcame its tendency to focus on the big customer and deliver second-class service to the others.

efforts. If there are any Harry-only tasks, Harry should do one of them. Otherwise, he should do another task.

This sort of distinction prevents Harry from expending his time on things that other employees can do, possibly causing a slippage of some Harry-dependent project.

The Advantages of Routines

Routines are an important compartmentalization strategy. If there are things that must be done regularly, they can be built into someone's schedule just as if they were appointments. This relieves a load on the scheduling question and allocates the required effort systematically.

For example, if you need to produce a monthly report, consider allocating time on the first Friday of every month to produce the previous month's report. This way, you won't habitually be trying to find time for this. By making it a routine rather than a project, you automatize the scheduling and reduce by one the number of decisions necessary. Most managers have enough decisions to make.

A special case where you may want to consider routines is the team meeting. It's often emphasized how expensive internal meetings are, in terms of the time costs of the participants. However, interruptions are expensive, too, and misunderstandings and errors more so. The more items a workplace is tracking, the more often it should hold brief team meetings. We've seen more than a few fast-moving groups that meet at the beginning of every day to share status, to allocate equipment, and otherwise to verify that everything is on track.

Smart Managing

Daily Meetings, Not Constant Interruptions

Managers who find themselves unable to keep up with a steady stream of interruptions and groups whose members are constantly stumbling over one another should consider regular morning meetings with the entire team.

In fast-moving workplaces, this can replace a good part of the manager's open-door time and can help prevent many sorts of errors and confusion. It can also contribute to team cohesion and morale.

Emotional Compartmentalization

Just allocating time and attention is not enough, though. There's also an emotional load associated with certain situations. If not managed appropriately, emotions can spill over to negatively affect a work group or an entire organization.

If you're upset about something, you must learn to compartmentalize that emotion. You must remain productive until the time and place arrives when you can focus on the situation producing the emotion and deal with it constructively. Being upset about something is no reason to go "off-task." This is true for each member of your work group.

Some people believe it's important, when they become upset, to deal with the upsetting issue or circumstance right away. Quite often this is a bad idea. A better course of action would be to defer the matter until the individuals involved can recover control of their emotions. Emotional upset is not a crisis. It should not be allowed to derail a carefully orchestrated work schedule.

The best advice here is just not to succumb. Learn the skill of emotional compartmentalization. Focus on the task at hand and set an example for your team. Encourage them to devote their full attention to whatever task they're working on and to trust that other situations will be dealt with in their due time and place. Then do whatever you must to fulfill that trust. Emotional situations cannot be ignored, but they cannot be allowed to take priority.

How to Compartmentalize

One fundamental objective of managing multiple projects is for every member of the team to know what to do next. When a piece of work is complete, it should be clear to the staff member what his or her next responsibility is. Another objective is to make maximum use of the most critical resource, usually a person on the team whose skills are in particularly high demand. A third objective is to ensure that every commitment is addressed in a timely fashion.

You're the person who must maintain these objectives. The best solution is particular to yourself, your group, and your responsibilities. Compartmentalization is a broad set of strategies that covers the middle ground of formality between PERT and "winging it." To compartmentalize effectively, you must answer at least the following questions:

- How many compartments should there be?
- How should you decide how to allocate attention among them?
- How much responsibility for this should you keep and how much should you delegate?

If you were to call us up and pay us our usual fees, we would proceed to help you think this through. Throughout this book, we've introduced ideas about the nature of work and the distinctions that can be made among tasks and projects. Some of these distinctions will be useful in planning your operation and others will not. Perhaps a single distinction—such as between your big customer and your other customers, or between internal and external work, or between desk work and field work—will clarify matters.

Understand, though, that every compartmentalization is a tradeoff. You're trading complexity for flexibility. A compartmentalization is a rule that relieves you of decisions.

For example, if you say you'll do office work on Mondays, you're limiting your capacity to do field work on that day and, as a result, you may lose some business. On the other hand, as a result of that constraint, you're gaining the guarantee that you'll be able to address your office work every week, without having to consider that aspect of your work every time you book an appointment in the field.

Similarly, if your critical resource, Harry, must do Harry-only work until his queue is empty, you may miss an opportunity for him to do lower-skilled work on a time-critical project. In exchange for missing this rare opportunity, you gain the confidence that Harry-only work is proceeding as efficiently as possible. (Notice that overriding your own rule in this case would not reduce your authority. Your rule is intended to be right most of the time, not all the time.)

As a rough rule of thumb, the more complicated your work allocation problem, the more of the complexity you may need to offload via compartmentalization.

Reducing Complexity Through Compartmentalization

What do these compartments do for us? They divide our one big problem into a collection of smaller, more tractable problems. We still must come up with a strategy for each of these smaller problems, to make sure that every item is addressed once it makes it into a compartment. The various compartments may have different strategies. (We'll have a lot to say about strategies that make sure you have airtight tracking systems in the next chapter.) The important thing to keep in mind is that everything needs to fit in somewhere.

It's best to avoid a miscellaneous category if you can. Above all, don't have a "fell behind the sofa" category. Make sure that everything is in some sort of queue and that everything will get timely attention.

Let's look at some of the ways we've already suggested to divide up tasks:

- Interruptible vs. concentrated
- Routine vs. occasional
- Can be done by only one person (Harry) vs. by several people
- On site vs. off site
- Main customer vs. other customers

It happens that each of these five ways of dividing tasks is based on a yes/no question. In principle, some questions may have several possible answers. However, even with just these five questions with two possible answers each, we already have 32 distinct possibilities. Do we really want to have 32 separate work queues?

That's missing the point. If you ask the questions in the right order, you can limit the number of categories.

First of all, routines are a special case and you need to deal with them first. A new routine is not a task or a project; it doesn't arrive at your door the way other requests arrive. A routine is a pattern that you extract from your observations of the operation and place into a particular time slot. Therefore, you should slot your routines into your team calendar first, with due consideration of who does what when. "Is this a routine?" is not a question that needs to be addressed for an incoming request.

Note that "interruptible time" is simply a routine for yourself, though it's an unusual one in that you may wish to have some other task to do in case no one interrupts you, a task that you can easily set aside if interrupted.

Some examples in this chapter may apply to your situation and many others may not. Perhaps there's a particular piece of equipment that you may or may not need to allocate. Perhaps you wish to track projects differently than individual tasks. Perhaps you wish to distinguish among tasks according to duration—short, medium, and long.

In your staff interviews, you got a complete list of everything your team members are doing. Your job is to find the right number of categories to track everything effectively, then to arrange the list of categories in a logical order for allocation of resources.

You may end up with a list like this:

- Routines
- Off-site projects
- Projects that require Harry

Adding a Routine

Smart Managing If a particular task seems to come up regularly, perhaps it should be added to a routine. For example, if someone requisitions graph paper every other week, that purchase might be moved to a standard weekly check for office supplies, where it would cause less disruption.

It's your job as manager to notice when tasks repeat often enough to be added to a routine. If a task is a true routine, it's worth paying careful attention to how it's done, to minimize cost and impact on workload.

- Projects that require the SuperGizmatron machine but not Harry
- Other projects
- Brief tasks

This list assumes a couple of things: Harry doesn't do off-site projects and Harry is more critical than the SuperGizmatron. Whatever categories you devise should fit the specific needs of your situation.

The important point is that you should avoid having too many categories. The purpose of the compartmentalization is to simplify your problem, not to cause confusion.

Moving Toward the Airtight System

In this chapter and several preceding it, we've been examining the question of managing the commitments of a work group. We've suggested using simplicity as your guiding principle as you decide what strategies to implement to manage your group's commitments.

We've recommended tools such as the to-do list and the calendar (in both personnel and project views). We've encouraged you to use interviews with staff members to get the big picture of your group's commitments and, in the process, to gain insight into individuals' perceptions and attitudes about the group and its work. We've suggested that reliance on prioritization is a symptom of larger problems and we've advocated for improved gatekeeping as a way to reduce instances where prioritization must take place.

Now, you've set up gatekeeping to control the flow of projects into your system. Next, you must control the activities that accomplish the projects to which you have committed. Compartmentalization is a key strategy for dividing attention among many responsibilities. The ability to compartmentalize is an important skill to learn, for your personal time management as well as for your allocation of tasks to staff members. Master these techniques and you'll approach your ultimate goal—an airtight system that performs reliably, directing attention to the right project at the right time and successfully delivering on every commitment, large or small.

Manager's Checklist for Chapter 10

❑ Reliability means every commitment gets its due attention.

❑ A high-functioning team puts great demand on the manager.

❑ Formal project management methods are designed for a small number of large projects. Workplaces with a large number of small projects need less formal, but airtight systems.

❑ One way to allocate attention systematically is to subdivide work into compartments. An important example is a manager dividing time into interruptible and concentrated time.

❑ The right system for compartmentalizing is different for every situation. It should be as simple as possible, yet include everything the team is doing.

"How Does It Know ...?": Tracking Systems

Consider the Thermos brand vacuum bottle—how does it know? It keeps hot drinks hot and cold drinks cold. Yet there's no embedded temperature sensing equipment. How does it know which to do?

A friend of ours finds this riddle very amusing. Of course, the answer is simple: the bottle doesn't know at all.

The solution to that riddle is a great example of the "as simple as possible" principle, from the Albert Einstein profundity that we cited to open Chapter 7: "Everything should be made as simple as possible, but no simpler." Although the bottle does not know what temperature to keep the beverage, the beverage itself knows its temperature and the bottle simply serves to prevent heat from leaking in or out.

Ideally, management is like a vacuum bottle. As a manager, you want to minimize your interaction with work that's going well. The last thing you want to do with a project that's proceeding smoothly is to risk arousing bad feelings, such as suspicion and defensiveness. On the other hand, if work is going badly, you want to be able to intervene in a timely and effective fashion.

Semi-formal systems move as much knowledge as possible from the plan to the work itself. The tracking system is distributed across the work. The work "knows" what it is doing and "knows" when to report itself off-track. Then, you can intervene, to keep the heat in or out of the particular delivery as needed.

About Tracking

There are at least five purposes for tracking work:

- To maintain a complete work inventory for accountability
- To know when to intervene
- To be able to respond to outside inquiries
- To improve group cohesion and morale
- To identify and correct recurring problems

Maintaining a Complete Inventory

We're developing a system where nothing gets dropped. To make sure nothing gets dropped, it's necessary to track everything.

Busy individuals can't be expected to keep all their commitments in their head. A busy group doesn't even have the luxury of a single brain to store all its commitments mentally. The fundamental principle of reliability is to track everything, without exception. For most individuals, formal tracking of commitments is extremely helpful. With the shared responsibilities of a workgroup, a formal tracking system is indispensable.

A related concept is *accountability*, a concept not directly related to financial accounting. A task is considered accountable if its completion is an obligation that one person makes to another, who may or may not be in a formal supervisory role. Some workplaces extend the idea of a complete task inventory to complete accountability. In this strategy, every single task achieved in the workplace by every member of the organization—including the CEO—is accountable to someone else.

Accountability has its costs. The demands on the time of the reviewer are inevitable, even if the reviews are usually very brief. A greater risk occurs when reviews are negative. Nonetheless, we recommend complete accountability for everyone who's not a sole practitioner. The impossibility of true accountability is a disadvantage of the soloist, who must provide an extra measure of self-discipline.

> **Key Term**
>
> **Accountability** Obligation to accept responsibility for a task or a project. A task or a project is considered accountable if there's another member of the organization (besides the person doing the work) who's designated to review the work. In some situations, the reviewer may have the power to decide not to review. Organizations where every single work item is accountable have high reliability, though efficiency may suffer and there are risks to morale as well.

The Founder's Timesheet

Here's a situation that we've seen time and again. An entrepreneurial service business has grown to the point where time reporting is perceived to be necessary. (Of course, we believe it's always necessary, even for the soloist! However, in the hubbub of a startup, this need is often missed.)

The founder designates an administrator to ensure that every employee always fills out a time sheet, with the penalty of "no time sheet, no paycheck" usually invoked as if it were a brilliant and unprecedented innovation.

The founder, however, is not used to filling out time sheets and generally has time that's particularly difficult to categorize. The founder sets up the administrative employee as the reviewer of all time sheets and is now forced to report to that person. We've seen this particular relationship fail in several companies.

It takes a very strong administrator to stand up to the boss time and time again, demanding the same accounting that the boss has demanded of everyone else, until the boss complies. It takes a strong boss to not merely tolerate but actually encourage the nagging that's necessary to resolve this problem. The company that successfully makes this transition is a strong one.

Knowing When to Intervene

We touched on this point in the introductory section. A system of tracking is more than an inventory system. It's a work status system. As individual projects slip, they may require management intervention. Sometimes extra resources are needed or anticipated skills aren't sufficient. This should be obvious to the production staff.

What they don't always understand, though, is that a late project may have resource or timing impacts on other work items that they don't know about. You need to know what's going on, not just to keep the sails trimmed and the rudder aimed, but to keep the ship on track and safe.

Being Responsive to Outside Inquiries

As a manager, you're expected to know the status of all work assigned to you, in case a customer, a supervisor, or a constituent needs this information for his or her own purposes.

In this case, it's important to distinguish between *active* and *potential* knowledge. In some situations, you may be expected to know the status of certain important work at any instant. This would be active knowledge. More typically, it's sufficient to set things up so that you know how to get the information on short notice. This is potential knowledge, enough for most managers in most workplaces.

> **Key Term**
>
> **Active knowledge** What you can state with confidence and without any recourse to outside help.
>
> **Potential knowledge** What you can easily find out, on short notice. Active knowledge is always a good thing, but for most management purposes potential knowledge is sufficient.

Improving Group Cohesion and Morale

In some workgroups, none of the members has a clear idea of what the others are doing. In such cases, increasing the mutual understanding among the staff may be very beneficial to building team cohesion.

Business often brings people together who might not otherwise choose to interact with each other. This can lead to some awkwardness at informal gatherings, like lunch breaks, elevator rides, and business trips. The more staff members know about each other's work, the more points of contact they'll have for starting conversations.

While it's not the only way to promote the formation of a group culture, mutual knowledge is useful in this regard. For this purpose, large group meetings are expensive and awkward. Visible tracking of status is an alternative. For example, for groups whose projects last days or weeks and have identifiable phases, it could be appropriate to use a large whiteboard or similar public display to show project status. Other displays could include sales figures, vacation calendars, and internal news.

There's a tradeoff here with aesthetics, so some may object. Whiteboards and corkboards may not be as pretty as paintings and posters. Another problem is that some information may not be suitable for all visitors.

However, just as something was lost when libraries moved to online catalogs from browsable index cards, something is lost with management software: team efforts may become less visible to team members. It may be worthwhile to put some effort into maintaining some public display of important status information.

Display Important Information to Staff

Smart Managing

Use your walls and cubicle exteriors to communicate with your team. Encourage people to display work products they're proud of. Use corkboards to display morale-building correspondence, the status of large products, and internal improvement initiatives. Be creative. The most useful information can vary dramatically from workplace to workplace.

This sort of display of work status can facilitate communication within your group. It also can help people exchange ideas that can improve your process. If there's a tracking method that you can make visible, use it to help the team understand the big picture of your current work.

Identifying and Correcting Recurring Problems

One reason to track everything is to identify problems, such as failed deliveries. Repeated problems are an opportunity for the manager to add value by intervening and for the staff to improve its skills. We will discuss this in detail in the next (concluding) chapter of this book. You can't resolve problems unless you can identify them. Often a simple change, like adding a daily delivery-check routine, can minimize recurring problems.

Compartmentalization and Tracking

In the previous chapter, we subdivided work into categories. Allocating parts of this category list to specific people went a good way toward ensuring that every commitment of the team eventually gets attention.

Each of the compartments may benefit from a separate strategy. Certainly, routines and multithreaded projects cannot be tracked in the same way. One of the main advantages of compartmentalization is to avoid a one-size-fits-all strategy for all your work.

Just remember that your compartmentalization must be exhaustive. Every piece of work must fit into one or another compartment. Otherwise your system develops a leak.

Keeping Track

The stresses of management bring out a lot of negative personality traits. We need to watch out for these tendencies in ourselves. One such tendency is toward what's known as "micromanagement" or, more informally, as the "control freak" tendency. This is the foolish idea that the only acceptable way to do anything is exactly the way we ourselves would do it. This drives a manager to indulge in random meddling and causes pointless stress all around.

On the other hand, staff members often perceive micromanagement when the manager isn't trying to control but merely to understand. We as managers need the big picture, but only the staff knows the components. We need to develop our asking skills and their answering skills.

Problems can come when talented people are inarticulate or lack confidence or simply have an artistic pride that doesn't want to reveal the chaotic state of a work in progress. Much of the solution to this problem can lie in formal processes that require specific check-ins at certain points. We'll have several examples later in this chapter.

As you go through these ideas, consider the optimum that you're aiming for. You want to extract the least amount of information needed to do an excellent job managing the entire team. This occasionally may mean discouraging endless reports from the chatty people on staff as well as encouraging elaboration from the taciturn.

It's actually best to formalize this process. Make work progress contingent on the minimal amount of reporting. Most people want to get their work done; if reporting is part of that job, they're more likely to comply.

There may be times when you want information, but the point at which you want it is not easily formalized. In this situation, consider the person who can provide that information. When is he or she most likely to want to share information with you? Try to make yourself available at that time. Often this will be just after the person has accomplished something. Making time for a staff member to brag about his or her accomplishments is, within reason, time well spent, especially with people who don't tend to talk very much. You'll learn more about them, their skills, and their interests if they get a chance to review their actions with you while those actions are fresh in their memory. They'll also appreciate the interest that you're showing in them at that time. If you wait until the experience is stale, though, they may find your inquiries intrusive and ill-timed.

Airtight Listing of Responsibilities

In Chapter 9, we stated that a fundamental component of a reliable work strategy is the ability to control the flow of incoming work—what we call "gatekeeping." As the gatekeeper, you have responsibility to make sure nothing gets dropped, starting from the moment the task or project comes through your gate.

The first step to making sure that nothing gets dropped is making sure that everything gets identified. Ideally, this is every single item, without exception. A foolproof system for identifying and tracking every item is what we call "airtight."

There's only one sort of exception in a reliable organization. That would be tasks that can be handled immediately. If someone calls you up and asks for your fax number or your mailing address, that's certainly a task, but it doesn't really need to be tracked because you handle it immediately.

However, every item that isn't handled immediately should be tracked somehow. The tracking, in principle, should be less difficult than the task itself. Lightweight tracking methods would include the task sheets we describe below or e-mail with a reply requested.

It's even more important to have a clear process for initiating a project and to have a clear distinction between a prospective project and an actual one. Remember the "only one priority" principle, as well, and be sure that your commitments to any internally generated projects are in your time budget and taken seriously.

Airtight Routines

A system for tracking routines is an almost automatic consequence of simply defining the routines. The list of routines is divided up so that each routine appears on a checklist. There are two steps to dividing up the routines into checklists.

First, distinguish among daily, weekly, monthly, etc. schedules for these routines. Each time cycle needs a separate checklist. For instance, daily items go on one list and weekly items on another.

Once you've completed the first pass, decide whether you'll need the help of more than one person to complete each list. If so, further divide the list into roles. For example, accounting data entry could be assigned to "clerk" and purchasing routines

Have Someone Check the Checklist

Oddly, some people may not know how to use a checklist. We once had an assistant who had an assigned set of weekly duties. She habitually and consistently dated and filled out the checklist we'd given her, checking off each activity that she did. We concluded that she was doing all the assigned work. Eventually it emerged that she wasn't and that she simply and forthrightly left the checkboxes for those activities unchecked.

This is an example of the accountability principle. A manager should have been looking at the checklists, rather than letting the employee simply file them. This check might have been occasional after the routines were established, but early on it needed to be detailed. A manager also should have checked the quality of the work.

to "purchasing agent." It's better to assign roles rather than names to the checklists, because routines need to be covered whether or not any particular person is available. Of course, you'll also be assigning the roles to particular people.

Don't forget to check the checklists! (See sidebar, "Have Someone Check the Checklist.")

Airtight One-Off Task Tracking

Recall that we refer to a single work item that can be done by a single person in a single effort as a "task." Almost every work group generates a steady stream of such tasks. In some groups, the manager assigns all tasks, but in others any member can make direct requests of any other member.

Here we describe a lightweight method for tracking such tasks, as well as small projects that a single person can complete. We've devised this low-technology approach to tracking individual tasks that many people have found very useful, the task sheet method.

Our method requires nothing more than a small three-part form. (A quarter-page will do.) The form contains a start date, a due date, the name of the requesting and the delegated parties, a client or project field, a description of the task, and a completed date field. (See Figure 11-1.)

REQUEST	
To:	From:
Start Date:	Due Date:
Client/ Project File:	
Task:	
	Date Done:

Figure 11-1. A simple task tracking form

Some groups create these task sheets on an ad hoc basis, others only at group meetings. The latter approach is helpful when there are frequent group meetings and much requesting going back and forth.

Let's call the person making the request the "requestor" and the person accomplishing the task the "delegate." The process begins with a verbal request from the requestor that meets with a verbal agreement by the delegate that the task is feasible by the proposed due date. (We assume that the delegate has a clear, ongoing estimate of his or her workload, so that the task is known to be feasible.)

The requestor fills out all the fields except the completed date and gives the top (white) copy to the delegate. The requestor then files the yellow copy under the appropriate date in a tickler file (actually a set of files, organized by date). The final (pink) copy is filed in the appropriate client or project file.

Normally, the work is completed on the due date or earlier. Upon timely completion of the work, the delegate submits the white copy to the requestor, who removes the corresponding yellow copy from the tickler file, staples the two copies together, and files them in the relevant client or project file.

The white copy of the form is thus a physical token of the task that the delegate passes back to the requestor upon completing the work.

The yellow copy serves as the tracking device. On a daily basis, the requestor can check the tickler files and retrieve any yellow sheets for tasks that were due on the previous day (or earlier). If the delegate did not finish the task, corrective action can then be taken. If the delegate finished the task but failed to follow the procedure, the manager should make it clear that the system's value is based on cooperation.

The pink copy of the form serves the purpose of potential knowledge. If a customer asks about the status of a request, it can easily be determined by looking in the customer's file. The presence of the pink copy in a file indicates that the task has been duly assigned, with its anticipated completion date. The presence of the stapled white and yellow copies verifies that the task has been completed.

Advantages and Disadvantages of the Task Sheet Method

The simple, low-technology, three-part form achieves most of the goals of tracking. It can be negotiated and completed in under a half minute and filed in another half minute. It leaves a trace so that it can be looked up if needed. It requires no mental or administrative load unless it becomes late, and it forces action only if the designated due date is missed.

This approach is very helpful in simplifying and civilizing the relationship between requestor and delegate in general—and it's especially helpful when the requestor is the delegate's supervisor.

All too often we see our managers passing off vague and ill-defined responsibilities to their assistants. The assigner then lies awake at night worrying about whether the task has been completed and will at some random time abruptly and urgently ask the assistant something like "Did you remember to fax the amendments to the Veeblefetzer contract?"

This is a clear no-win situation, because the assistant will inevitably react defensively. If the work is not done, the response will be something like "You didn't tell me that was important." If it is done, the response will be more like "Don't you trust me? You asked me not to bother you about things that don't need further attention from you!"

The task sheet method avoids this no-win situation. The delegate has the pleasure of announcing completion of a task and the requestor has no responsibility to query or intervene until the paperwork indicates that something has gone wrong.

The main disadvantage of the task sheet method is one that is common to all process improvement methods. It adds to the workload before it delivers meaningful results. It's incumbent on a manager adopting this or any other process improvement method to insist on compliance—and to set a good example.

Everyone who uses this system to delegate tasks must check the tickler files diligently and must deal with failures

---

Task Sheet Database

The task sheet is a low-tech tool that delivers powerful results. However, if you're working to reduce reliance on paper systems, it may seem like a step backward.

A simple database can be easily constructed to mimic this system. Using the task sheet in Figure 11-1 as your model, set up a database form with the appropriate fields. Then, create find/sort routines that generate reports that take the place of the three parts of the paper form.

- Each delegate will want to view all his or her active task commitments. This list should be arranged by due date. (This takes the place of the white copy.)
- Each requestor will want to view all his or her active task requests. (This takes the place of the yellow copy.)
- Anyone might want to view active task requests for a particular customer. This serves as potential knowledge, enabling anyone to answer a customer's question about the status of a request. (This takes the place of the pink copy.)

immediately, calmly, and responsibly. Everyone who is delegated tasks must keep track of the task sheets and hand them in upon completing the tasks.

Task Size and Trust

How large a project can be handled using the task sheet method? Similarly, how large a chunk of work should be treated as a single item in the workflow of a project?

According to our definition of a task, an item taking more than a single workday to complete shouldn't be called a task. Nevertheless, it may not be necessary to track the progress of a person working on a multi-day delivery every day. Should such an activity get a single task sheet or be identified as a single item on a project schedule?

This depends on the level of trust you've established with the staff member assigned. A good management rule of thumb is that it's much easier to grant authority than to revoke it. The consequence is that you should begin your relationship with an employee by following his or her progress closely and then backing off gradually.

A good approach is to set up particular milestones in each assignment and have each team member report as they pass each one. Set up as many milestones as you need to be

Setting Milestones

As we mentioned in Chapter 5, a milestone is a well-defined intermediate point in the delivery of a project. You determine the milestones of a project, primarily to track whether the project is behind schedule, on schedule, or ahead of schedule.

In large-scale project management, a milestone is often set at points where multiple threads coalesce into a single thread and some formal reviews are performed. However, you may set as many milestones as you wish. If there's an urgent project that you're having trouble tracking, it may be less intrusive to your staff to set multiple milestones when they should briefly report to you, rather than to frequently interrupt them to ask, "How's it going?"

TRICKS OF THE TRADE

comfortable that you know how things are proceeding. As you come to trust a staff member's work, you may need few or no milestones within a work effort.

Airtight Projects

The points that we brought out in discussing the task tracking system apply to any project tracking system that's worth its salt. Projects are much more complicated than tasks, so there are many ways to track them. However, the following principles apply:

- **Exhaustiveness:** Have a complete list of your commitments.
- **Minimal overhead:** Have your tracking be as small a part of the work as possible.
- **Minimal intrusion:** Try to keep out of the way when things are going well.
- **Potential knowledge:** Have quick ways to find out what is going on.
- **Early warning:** If things are behind schedule, have ways to know it.
- **Compliance:** Full cooperation is required—or else the effort is wasted.

The Job Jacket

A method very commonly used to track projects is the "job jacket" or "job folder." This is a physical document with the plan for the project that's passed from station to station. A copy is kept by the manager who made the assignments. A sort of moving checklist is affixed to the folder; any documentary materials associated with the work are passed along inside the folder. It's especially common in environments where the individual stages are brief and there are numerous handoffs.

The job jacket approach manages minimal overhead and minimal intrusion. It's less than perfect as potential knowledge, because in principle a manager seeking information has to follow the project through its entire designated path. What's worse, informal job swapping among staff members can make the manager lose the thread entirely.

The simple job jacket system also has no early warning system built in. The manager will not know if a work is off track until someone in the production chain takes the trouble to admit it.

> **Job jacket** A method for tracking projects (also known as a job folder), in which a physical folder is created and developed for each project. The first document in the job jacket is the planned sequence of activities; it's usually attached to the folder or written onto a form printed on the folder. A copy is kept by the manager who made the assignments. As the project progresses from phase to phase, the job jacket is passed along with it. Documents generated along the way are added to the folder. It constitutes physical evidence of the progress of the project.

Baton-Passing Strategies

It's possible to resolve the deficiencies of the job jacket method by adding a little bit of overhead at certain milestones. In some circumstances, this is achieved by an extra check-in at the points when the project moves from hand to hand.

There are a number of ways to do this. One is to simply set up the process so that all deliverables pass from employee to employee only through the manager. For example, instead of moving from you to Alice to Bob to Carol to David and back to you, the project could move from you to Alice to you to Bob to you to Carol to you to David and back to you. We call this the "star system," because the path taken by the project is conceptually shaped like an asterisk. (See Figure 11-2.)

> **Star system** A baton-passing system where the manager reviews and controls the project after every step in the process. So named because of the conceptualized shape of the progress of the project, the star system maximizes managerial involvement, but it's impractical in situations where individual project steps are brief. It's rarely used because it ties the manager too tightly to the process.

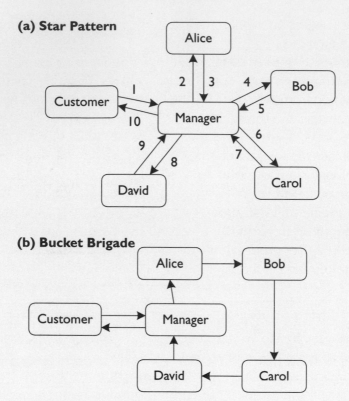

Figure 11-2. Baton-passing strategies
One way to make sure the manager has maximum information about a project is to pass the job along in a "star" pattern (a) rather than the more conventional "bucket brigade" pattern (b). Arrows show examples of how control flows.

Obviously, this system puts too many burdens on you if each step is a quick one. You would then be handling each project more or less constantly. On the other hand, if each project changes hands only every few days, this method becomes feasible. The star system also gives you the chance to change course frequently. The team may not know their assignments until the last minute. You get more flexibility this way, at the cost of more work for you and less perceived predictability on the part of the staff.

In practice, this system is rarely used because it places too much demand on the availability of the manager. The manager is not free to be unavailable for any extended period or the process stops.

A less extreme approach is simply to enforce some communication with you at each step. In many situations, an e-mail message can do the trick: Alice finishes her task, e-mails you a status report, and passes the project to Bob. In other environments, a publicly displayed whiteboard can show the status of each project: Bob finishes his task, marks the status on the board, and passes the project to Carol. Unlike the method where everything passes through the manager, this approach has the disadvantage that employees can easily forget or ignore it: Carol passes the project to David and neither updates the tracking system. You'll need to offer persuasion and incentive to get this to work.

An intermediate approach can be used if a computer file can replace the physical job jacket. In this case, you can base your tracking on a policy that each intermediate deliverable must be a file or set of files meeting a certain specification and placed in a certain directory under a certain name. The act of passing the work along then leaves a trail which you or any authorized person on the project can follow.

Airtight Multithreaded Projects

All of the above discussion is based on the idea of a single-threaded project. If work is split into multiple threads, the job jacket system is obviously inadequate. How should a project be tracked when there are two or more simultaneous sequences of operations?

If complex multithreading is common, some centralized control may be necessary. That is, you may need to use the star system approach, since it may be difficult for production staff to keep track of the many streams of work and their contingencies.

In the simpler case, where work breaks into a small number of threads that reunite, you may wish to devise a simple extension of a job jacket system. In this system, the primary job jacket stays with the critical path thread (that is, the sequence of events that determines the minimum delivery time), but two extra tasks are added to that thread. Borrowing the computer jargon used in parallel programming, we'll call them *fork* and *join*.

The concept is simple. Whenever a project thread splits into two or more threads, we add a fork. Whenever two or more threads come together, we add a join.

The fork task creates a new job jacket. Then, for this forked subproject, do whatever tracking you would normally do for a project. While active, the forked subproject is tracked as a separate project. When it reaches completion, the forked project is delivered to the person responsible for the join operation, but it's not marked complete.

> **Fork** The moment when a project thread is split into two or more threads. From that point on until the threads join, two streams of work are operating in parallel on that project.
>
> **Join** The moment when two or more project threads come together. It occurs when a production step depends on the output of both processes.
>
> In simple multithreaded projects, the equivalent of a second project may be generated at each fork and terminated at each join. This allows for tracking multithreaded projects much as you would track single threads.

When the join task occurs on the critical path, the expectation is that the forked process should be complete. The person responsible for the join does the standard project completion protocols for an internal project (if any), then begins work on the next phase or passes the work on, as appropriate.

This expedient of a temporary subproject that's treated like any other project allows you to handle a multithreaded project in a straightforward way, without complex project management strategies. There's simply an extra job jacket that pops into existence for a short time, so the subproject is tracked like any other job.

Sequencing Strategies

Projects have deadlines. The order in which projects are to be completed is not necessarily the order in which they come in.

To make matters worse, a project passed from hand to hand in a strict queuing system can often sit in several in-boxes before it reaches completion.

The prioritization bug bites people when they accept too many projects and they're constantly shuffling items around in great urgency trying to get everything to fit. Let's again use the quote from Albert Einstein as a touchstone: "Everything should be made as simple as possible, but no simpler."

It's much simpler to do everything in the order it comes in. Is that "as simple as possible"? Or is it "simpler"? The strategy of first-in first-out works perfectly in some situations, but not in all.

Sometimes a high-valued, fast-turnaround project will be accepted on short notice. If you've been doing adequate gate-keeping, this project is doable without disrupting any other deliveries. However, this project can't be delivered on time if it waits its turn.

But it's also not possible to invert the sequence and always work on the project that's due soonest. In that case, high-load projects will be ignored and crisis will ensue.

Unfortunately, there's no hard-and-fast answer to the question of sequencing projects. It's your job as manager to decide what order will allow your team to meet all the demands. You'll need to think and plan carefully. You'll need to keep everything in mind so that each member can concentrate on one thing at a time. This, in turn, is why you need the best information you can get at all times.

When and Whether to Computerize

Many of the suggestions we've been making can be implemented by using features of standard networked software products. Groupware products such as Microsoft Outlook, Lotus Notes, and Novell GroupWise support a considerable level of scheduling and task tracking, so that you may not need to resort to the complexity of full-blown project management software. For groups with in-house capacity to develop software, a customized system is not unreasonable.

Know Your Software

Smart Managing Many workgroups, perhaps most, dramatically underuse their software capabilities. There's general confusion about how deeply any individual should study and understand any one piece of software—particularly since almost everyone has access to more software than he or she could realistically learn to use to full effect.

As a manager, you should focus on understanding the capacity of the software that you've already purchased. You don't need to understand the details. Once you've built some procedures that you feel comfortable with and understand the tools you have available, it can be a good idea to contract with a computer consultant to take you to the next level. A consultant can design a robust software solution using the tools you have available and already understand.

Even spreadsheets like Microsoft Excel can be adapted to track projects and deliverables. (If you take this approach, please read up on the "shared" attribute of Excel spreadsheets and understand why it's necessary.)

It's been our experience that very few work groups take advantage of the potential of the software systems they have available. The complexity barrier presented by much contemporary software is responsible for this double waste of productivity. (Neither the users of the software nor its designers are fully realizing their productive potential in this situation!) Whether it's appropriate in any given case to overcome this barrier depends on the group, its needs, its skills, and the tools available to it.

Software can allow you to implement an airtight management system that's both more pleasant to maintain and more powerful than any paper system. Unfortunately, standard methods have not yet emerged in groupware. Not only is every workgroup different, but there are many software environments in which they operate.

Tracking Closes the Loop

In Chapter 3 of this book, we considered how a degree of for-malism (especially as implied by the presence and use of forms) increases a workplace's productivity and efficiency. The recommendations we've made about tracking in this chapter arise from the understanding that tracking, while perhaps an unwelcome sign of formalism, is critical to that productivity and efficiency. The workplace that lacks a system for tracking com-mitments and handoffs will be disorganized. Likewise, a work-place with bad systems will not function at its best. A tracking system that is intrusive or adds significant overhead without producing significant benefits is a bad system.

The systems you institute must be appropriate, adequate to the need, but not excessive. Such a tracking system will open a window on the complexity of your workplace, allowing you to better understand and control what goes on there. In the next (concluding) chapter, we'll discuss in detail how to make changes to your systems.

Manager's Checklist for Chapter 11

❑ Your goal is to develop a system where nothing gets dropped. To do so, everything must be tracked. Formal tracking of commitments is extremely helpful and, in a workgroup with shared responsibilities, indispensable.

❑ You, as the manager, need to know what's going on so that you can respond to inquiries about status, intervene before a task slips far off track, and identify and correct recurring problems.

❑ Expending your energy to keep track of your group's com-mitments is not "micromanaging" or "being a control freak." It's simply doing your job as a manager.

❑ The ideal tracking system allows airtight tracking of responsibilities, whether they're routines, one-off tasks, or projects.

❏ Pay attention to how the baton is passed as each task in a
project sequence is completed. The completion of a task is
information you may want access to at any time. You may
choose to have individuals check in with you as they pass
milestones or to have them simply note the change in status where you can look it up. Some groups use a computer program to track projects.

How to Change
a System

In this book, we've introduced a way of thinking that's somewhat abstract. Our consulting work takes us into a wide range of scenarios and workplaces, and this sort of abstraction helps us to extract general insights from a broad range of specifics.

Your problems, however, are specific. To get full value from our abstractions, you'll need to fit them back to the specifics of your situation. The specifics are up to you—and you need to plan them with care.

Because people are complicated creatures, workgroups are complicated systems. The best plans often go astray when many people are involved. As you plan to implement some of our suggestions in your workgroup, please understand that changing systems can be a frustrating process, however worthwhile the outcome.

It's best to get things right the first time, of course, but it's not always possible. Complicated changes are difficult to get right. The bigger and more important the change, the less likely you'll succeed immediately. If you make a major change, you should anticipate that you will not get the details perfect. You'll need to tune your new system as you go along.

This, unfortunately, increases the duration of unproductive but necessary activity as you modify the new ways of doing things in order to cope with unforeseen problems. Continual change without substantial results reduces the credibility of the change process.

Beginnings are especially critical. If you're planning to implement major changes, be very careful about how and when changes are implemented.

Timing Major Changes

If a major overhaul is needed, the following would be a good overall strategy:

- Establish credibility with small changes.
- Make the case for change, on an ongoing basis.
- Compartmentalize and make an overall plan.
- Begin a design of a reliable subsystem for each compartment.
- Present your preliminary ideas to the team.
- Revise the plan based on team input and announce a changeover date.

We'll discuss these steps in turn below.

Increasing Formality Equals Change

In some places, the formality of the procedures we suggest may in themselves constitute a major change. This particular change is one that managers can put in place without much staff input, because the extra work falls to the manager, not to the production staff. However, the formalism of meetings, changeover dates, and rule books may be unexpected.

Handled with good humor, this formalism need not be intimidating. Rather, it can serve as an example of the sort of clarity and precision that the group needs to strive for to achieve its full potential. If your workgroup reacts as if allergic to formality, you might encourage the affected individuals to read and discuss Chapter 3 with you.

Establish Credibility with Small Changes

Aim for early success. That's a simple rule of thumb in establishing credibility as a change agent. Go after the proverbial "low-hanging fruit." As you consider your entire operation systematically, you should keep alert for the simplest change that could make the most difference.

Look for consistent, nagging problems that seem as though they could be resolved with just a little effort. These should not be problems that are specific to a particular person or a few people, as those can be particularly hard to resolve. Rather, try to identify snags that come up constantly for many people on the team. These are problems that often can be dramatically resolved with a little creative thought.

Almost every group develops some silly counterproductive habits that can be changed to great effect, enhancing the reputation of the change agent. If you've been part of the group for a long time, you may be as unaware of these as anyone else. It's a good idea, then, to bring in outside reviewers during the early stages of a change campaign. Perhaps someone else new to the environment will notice something as simple as a lack of personal mail slots.

Make the Case for Change

A great deal has been written on the subject of change within organizations. One prominent book

> **Low-Hanging Fruit**
>
> It may be a cliché, but clichés emerge because of some underlying wisdom.
>
> Change in an organization is difficult and risky but can have huge payoffs. A key to success is establishing your credibility as an agent of change. The best way to begin doing so is by identifying relatively easy changes with relatively large payoffs. These are the "low-hanging fruit" or the "easy pickings." Prove that things can get better by starting with an endeavor that's likely to succeed and make a significant difference. Delay the really big changes until you've proven that small changes can work.
>
> **Smart Managing**

Some Sweet Fruit Hangs Very, Very Low

An extreme example of an easy but important change we ran into was a successful talent agency whose entire staff had never worked in any other business setting. One major complaint was that they had a lot of trouble keeping track of internal communications. In many businesses, such a complaint might indicate a complicated tracking and filing problem—but not so in this one.

It turned out that no one had ever set up mail slots for the staff, so papers were being left randomly on desks and chairs because there was no method set up for exchanging documents. In this case, a capital expenditure of $18 dramatically improved the situation.

on the subject is cheerfully entitled *Why Change Doesn't Work* by Harvey Robbins and Michael Finley (Princeton, NJ: Peterson's, 1996). All those books about change are cogent evidence that it's harder to redesign an organization than to design an entire organization from a blank slate.

Change definitely involves effort. But you wouldn't have read this far into the book if you didn't think it was worth the effort, of course. Your commitment to change is not enough, though. All of the members of your staff will need to make some effort if the change is to be successful. In order to achieve this, you need to convince each of the members, one at a time, that the effort is worth making.

This amounts to a marketing and sales campaign. Your product—the newly systematic workgroup—has substantial benefits in the form of less stressful work and more reliable results in the long run, but it also has costs in the form of efforts needed to understand new ways of proceeding and to change habits. There will also, almost inevitably, be an adjustment period as unforeseen problems plague the new system.

While a few major internal presentations may help move this process along, your best bet is to be constantly promoting the idea of improved systems well in advance of putting the changes in place. But be careful about going too far. You'll lose credibility if you talk about changes for years without implementing any. A few months' advance notice is best.

In particular, the approaches we suggest rely heavily on the ability of the team to predict how long any given task will take any particular person to whom it is assigned. This is especially critical for gatekeeping, where new work is accepted or declined (or at least encouraged or discouraged) based on the current commitment level of the team. Although ultimate responsibility for these estimates lies with you, you'll probably need to draw heavily on the experience of your staff members to obtain these estimates, as we discussed in Chapter 8.

Many production staff members resist such estimation procedures. You'll need to explain why any estimate is better than none and why such estimates are critical to the overall performance of the organization. You'll need to explain why careful timekeeping is equally critical, to compare estimates with results. You'll need to convince everyone that the results will be worth the effort.

It may be much easier to get buy-in from your team if you understand the social structure of the team. Every workgroup has an opinion leader or two. It's rare that the manager and the opinion leader are the same person. (If you are In that fortunate position, this advice doesn't really apply to you.) If you can identify the opinion leaders, you have a point of leverage with the team. You need to apply special efforts to get the people whose opinions count the most to support what you're doing. If you have the support of the opinion leaders, others will follow. (Our thanks go to Madison, Wisconsin-based change consultant Trip Royal for this very useful advice.)

Get Buy-in from Opinion Leaders

Smart Managing

Buy-in from staff is critical to the success of internal changes. Change consultant Trip Royal recommends that you identify the opinion leader or leaders among your staff. An opinion leader is usually a popular person with whom others identify and whom they tend to emulate.

If you can identify an opinion leader in the group to be affected by a change you're proposing, approach that person individually and ask for support. If your overture is successful, that can go a very long way toward bringing the entire team on board.

Compartmentalize and Make an Overall Plan

Systems should not be changed haphazardly or under pressure. You need to make time in your own schedule for planning and implementing changes.

You may not need to make all the changes at once. Compartmentalization is a way to stage the changes. You can make changes in each subdivision of your workload as needed, focusing on the areas most in need of change.

If you intend to use our compartmentalization approach, the first step may be setting up the compartmentalization. Staff members need to understand that each piece of work needs to fall into one or another category and that each category will have its own set of rules. For this to happen, you need to clarify to yourself how work is divided. The rules should be as clear as possible. One good way to help clarify the sorting of tasks is rules formed like the following: "If you are uncertain whether a job is type A or type B, always choose type B."

Rules are tools to reduce decision-making. A group that makes decisions consistently (Bob always comes to the same conclusion as Ted or Alice would, faced with the same decision) performs consistently. That consistency is essential to reliability. Rules are not unnecessary formalism—they are shortcuts to reliability.

Once you've defined your compartmentalization, you need to plan a sequence of changes so that each compartment can be made as formal as necessary to maintain airtight reliability. The sequence of changes to choose is affected by many factors.

Two somewhat contradictory factors tend to promote starting with a particular change:

- Changes that are most dramatically needed should be made earlier than those with smaller benefits.
- Changes that are more likely to be successful should be put in place before those that are higher risk.

Usually these factors will pull in opposite directions. When they don't, you have a "low-hanging fruit" project that you can

---

Managerial Compartments

Entrepreneurs and managers of small businesses, this one's for you. If you're having difficulty naming the compartments for which you're responsible, try this. Divide a sheet of paper into four columns, then write these headings above each column. As you review your responsibilities and commitments, assign them to one of these compartments. You'll find very little on your plate that you can't assign to one of these general headings:
• Finance
• Administration
• Marketing
• Personnel
   Circle the largest existing problem in each of the four categories. Then rank those in priority. You now know where to start on your process of continual improvement.

---

use to establish credibility, as described above.

Note, by the way, that sequencing change efforts is a fine example of prioritization used correctly. You will determine which changes need to be done in what order as a prioritization step. Then you will allocate time and resources for the earliest step or steps. At that point, the change is a commitment; although the delivery is internal, the commitment should be treated with the same respect as any external commitment.

In a major change effort based on compartmentalization, you should endeavor to step through each identified compartment of your workload once. This sequence constitutes an overall plan.

Change doesn't stop once you've made a first pass at each compartment, though. One management style that can be very successful divides the management effort into two parts. The first is maintaining the regular flow of work and the second is addressing the largest existing problem at any time. This results in a process of continual improvement.

Schedule and Plan Particular Changes

Any particular change will not affect everyone equally. The best time to implement a change is when the people who will be most impacted by that particular change are in a slack period. If your workplace is seasonal, you may be able to plan for these changes in advance. If your workplace is driven by customer demand, you may wish to cut back on marketing and promotions that affect a particular type of work so as to occasion enough slack to allow employees to devote attention to the change.

Sometimes, the nature of a change is such that new systems and old systems must be in place simultaneously, as in-progress projects clear the system under the old procedures. If this is the case, consider carefully whether any particular problems will arise as a result. Find specific ways to address these problems. Be sure that whatever you come up with isn't more confusing or less reliable than the system that's already in place. It may be necessary to tolerate some extra overhead during the transition period.

It may be at the busiest times that the need for a change is most evident. There may be pressure to implement the new system as early as possible, so as to have an impact on a current crisis.

Doing so is almost always a mistake. Changes implemented at a busy time are less likely to be fully understood and implemented. The extra effort needed to ensure that everyone affected makes the change correctly may not be available. Worse still, the change process will distract from the current urgent deliverables.

Even if a new procedure will be less time-consuming than the current one, it will require concentrated effort. This is reflected in the overall capacity of the people who need to implement the change. For substantial change efforts, even timesaving changes should be scheduled to occur when the workload is relatively light.

Remember the purposes of the redesign of each work compartment:

- **Completeness**, maintaining an unambiguous list of commitments
- **Gatekeeping**, keeping the whole set of commitments realistic
- **Tracking**, making progress visible

- **Accountability**, subjecting all work to possible internal review
- **Non-interference**, minimizing the system's overhead for on-track work
- **Correction**, catching and correcting problems as soon as possible
- **Estimation and verification**, estimating workload and improving estimation skill

> ### Changes Take Time
>
> The pressure to make changes is often strongest at times of crisis. However, such times are also the times when the change effort is least likely to succeed. Other responsibilities will interfere with the change effort, so it's likely to be implemented incompletely.
>
> Even timesaving changes take mental effort and emotional commitment. Changes should be scheduled during work lulls, not during times of peak demand.

These principles are universal. How these goals will be achieved, however, depends on the nature of the work, the people, and the resources.

Present Your Preliminary Ideas to the Team

At this point, it's time to put to the test your efforts to get buy-in from the team in principle, as you offer specific suggestions for improving the function of some particular aspect of your work. Draw up a specific list of suggestions for a particular work compartment, prepare it in writing, and distribute it in advance of a meeting of all affected personnel.

To begin the meeting, describe your rationale for your proposed changes. Then ask for input. It's a good idea at such a meeting to ensure that every person present voices an opinion.

Your suggestions may be technical or otherwise related to the specifics of your work product. They may also be systems-related, achieving the objectives listed in the previous section. Staff members with no management experience may have more difficulty understanding the systems-related changes than the technical changes, so the systems changes may require additional justification.

The types of workgroup to which the methods of this book apply best are ones that provide high added-value services. This being the case, the members of your team are probably intelligent and perceptive. Though they may not know much about management, they understand the nature of the work and the overall objectives of the organization. They may have a great deal of valuable insight to add to your initial proposals. They may have valid objections as well.

Do tolerate a certain level of hair-splitting arguments in this discussion. People who raise such objections are often the ones with a bent for clear, systematic thinking. If they have objections, ask them for realistic fixes, rather than trying to brush off their objections. Don't let the meeting get bogged down in particulars, though. If a particular point goes on too long, take it up after the meeting with the main interested parties.

This is not the time to exercise authority, though it may be appropriate to use the occasion to provide a gentle hint that you have some authority that you may need to exercise later.

Revise Your Plan in Detail

Based on the input from the meeting and whatever follow-up conversations you deem appropriate, draft a complete description of your planned changes. Even if your organization has tended toward informality in the past, describe the proposed rules as completely and precisely as the group culture will accept, read, and understand.

Don't get legalistic, though. Many companies have a "policy and procedure" manual that's of significance only in legal battles. The staff members who have agreed to its terms, implicitly or explicitly, are unlikely to have read it or passed it along to their own counsel to check.

If your organization has such a legal document, beware. Your procedures are to be written somewhere, but that isn't the place, unless you're prepared to get legal assistance.

It's a good idea to have a set of procedures for getting work done, in writing and amended as necessary. It should be short enough and clear enough to be understood in its entirety. Everyone should be encouraged to be alert for any ambiguities, contradictions, and archaisms in that rule book. It should be kept clear and current. The definitive copy should be on your computer network. Any changes should be announced. If you don't have a clear statement of your work rules, you can't expect people to reliably follow them.

Distribute the final copy of your proposed amendments to the rule book to all affected parties, along with a date on which the changes will become effective. Ask for assistance primarily on clarity and presentation, but allow for people to catch fundamental flaws. This step will help ensure that your changes work at least on paper.

> ### The Rule Book
>
> In addition to any formal policies and procedures manual issued by the HR department in collaboration with an army of attorneys, you should have a place where the day-to-day operational procedures of your workgroup are noted. Having a written operational guide can resolve ambiguities and help new staff members get on track.
>
> You should go to some trouble to keep the book current and clear and to make sure that the most current copy is available to anyone, either on a publicly accessible shelf or on a shared volume on your computer system.

Fix any mistakes and make necessary small changes a week in advance of the change date. Distribute it, along with any supporting documents such as new or replacement forms. If it's feasible, do a dress rehearsal of the procedures. Remind everyone of the date that the new policy takes effect.

At this point, you've done your best to get buy-in. It's now time to exert your authority.

Implement

On the date of the policy change, remind all people affected by it. Unless they ask you to review the changes, don't make any particular fuss about it. Act on the presumption that everyone knows what to do.

However, you should make a particular effort to be present and available when a new procedure takes effect. Do whatever you can to ensure that your understanding of how things are to proceed matches that of the participants in the process.

If you've prepared the ground correctly, the new procedures will immediately take root.

Tune and Follow Through

Your work as a change agent does not end at the moment that the new policy is put into place. In fact, the early days of the new policy are a critical test of the policy and of you as a change agent. Be sure to allocate a significant proportion of your time during the transition to ensure that things are proceeding smoothly and correctly.

Following the date of the change, here are some of the actions you will need to take:

- Ensure compliance
- Deal with unanticipated cases
- Identify snags
- Verify results

Ensuring Compliance

The joke has it that there's not much difference between theory and practice—at least, that is, in theory.

No matter how successful you've been in getting staff members to buy into your new approaches in theory, that doesn't necessarily guarantee their cooperation in practice. In the very early stages, you need to ensure that they all understand the new ways of doing things. A well-designed policy will have relatively little room for misinterpretation, but if the procedure is necessarily complex, you may be unable to achieve this ideal.

Early phases of a new procedure are a good time to identify flaws in your specification. If people are not doing things correctly, so as to support the intended goals of the change, this may indicate a communication problem. Do what you can to identify the nature of the miscommunication, then modify or

> ## ASAP Is Not a Due Date
>
> Recall the task sheets that we introduced in the previous chapter. These are intended to allow for reliable tracking of individual work tasks not associated with a larger project. The formal structure of a task sheet includes a due date and one copy is filed by date, so that overdue tasks can be identified.
>
> We have seen people mark "as soon as possible" on task sheets. Those who do so are clearly not thinking about those who need to file or retrieve the copy that's to be filed by date. Leaving aside the clarity or ambiguity of "ASAP" as a date for delivery, it's obviously not an acceptable date for filing and tracking purposes.
>
> Depending on the person, you can attempt to explain the reasons—or you can simply assert that only a day and a month can appear in this field on the form. A person who doesn't understand how this "date" causes the system to fail may feel that you're being unreasonable or inflexible, but a specific date is, of course, absolutely necessary.

clarify the rule specification to put an end to that particular misunderstanding. A common misunderstanding is the types of information that are required on a procedural form or record.

Another reason for compliance problems is that people are slow to change and quick to revert to old habits. Changes must be constantly reinforced in the early phases, until new habits develop. (A rule of thumb is that an action needs to be performed daily for about two months before it becomes habitual.) Therefore, you should not be surprised if some people are not cooperating with the newly instituted policy, at least at first. It's far easier to agree in principle to a major shift in the way things are done than to accept and adopt it in practice.

Dealing with Unanticipated Cases

It's unlikely that, even with your best efforts, you'll have thought of every implication of your new system. Consequently, you'll probably need to keep a close eye on the changed part of your operation for some time. Above all, it's important that items that slipped through the cracks in your original design not slip through the cracks in operation.

This is something to watch for in your overall compartmentalization of the work. It's not always clear in which category to
put a particular effort. If you're aiming at an airtight system, you
can't have stray items that don't fall under any protocol at all. To
a historically informal organization, this aspiration may sound
extreme. To soften the blow, it may help to remind them that
your goal is information, not micromanagement.

Encourage staff members to note any situations that don't
seem to be covered by the new policy. If these situations can be
resolved by clarifying the policy, do so. If the situations require a
minor change to policy, make such changes. If the situations
indicate a major omission in the rules, it may be necessary to
propose an amendment at a meeting and solicit comments
before making any permanent repairs.

Identifying Snags

Similarly, be open to staff complaints about steps in the process
that are too unwieldy. It may be that a step you envisioned as
taking a few seconds actually takes several minutes

Time Sheets

Careful and accurate time reporting is critical to the health
of a high-value service organization. Only accurate time reporting allows you to verify whether your projections and plans were appropriate, whether your rates support your work, and ultimately whether
to pursue, maintain, or abandon a particular line of business.

Time sheets also offer an opportunity for plugging leaks in your cat-
egorization of work. A particular category of time called "uncertain"
should be one of the options for logging time. This would be chosen if
the time does not fit into any of the established numbered categories.
Staff should be encouraged to use the "uncertain" category in case of
doubt.

As a manager, you should regularly review use of the "uncertain"
category on your staff's timesheets. You may discover a new category
of activity emerging or a misunderstanding about existing compartments. An employee who logs 10% of her time as "uncertain" is probably using the system appropriately; if that percentage creeps closer to
20%, you're seeing a sign of a problem.

or more in some cases, interfering with work progress.

If such a case comes up, you'll need to verify that staff members understand the purpose of the step. Also, make sure that the member with the complaint knows how much information you're expecting; sometimes employees comply with new procedures to excess. If he or she understands correctly, examine your own understanding. Is the step substantially more difficult than you anticipated? Is the staff member resisting because the step is really time-consuming or simply because the step is unfamiliar and perceived as unpleasant?

If the step is not overwhelmingly difficult but merely unpleasant, try to find some way to make the process more tolerable. For example, a document that's designed well can be remarkably more pleasant to work with than a document that's formatted poorly and therefore confusing.

If the step is genuinely too complicated, consider the possibility that you've made an error in design. Determine whether some other approach could achieve most or all of the same purposes without demanding as much time from the workers who are having difficulty.

Verifying Results

Finally, and most importantly, keep in mind the reasons for making those changes. You had specific objectives. How well are you achieving them? Has the effort been worthwhile? Is your tracking more effective? Do you have a clearer idea of what's going right and, more important, what's going wrong?

If not, why not? What can you do about it?

Effective Amendment

Be prepared for criticism. It's difficult to get these things right in one shot. Encourage feedback from the members of your team—and be open to their suggestions. The new policy is to improve operations, not to show what a great manager you are. Just as you and your employees work as a team, you should approach changes as a team effort. Don't let your improvements cause problems by being reluctant or unwilling to accept and consider feedback. Express your interest in criticism and suggestions—and mean it.

On the other hand, don't act too quickly. You must make changes carefully and with planning. Changes to changes are even more sensitive. Too many rounds of change in the same area of the business make it much harder for the team to adapt and weaken your credibility. If you need to amend your new policy, it's better to make larger changes rarely than to constantly tinker with smaller changes.

The Reliable Workgroup

As you can see, there's no universal recipe for success in establishing reliability in the workplace. In this book we've aimed at giving you food for thought and a vocabulary with which to do the thinking.

As a manager, you'll succeed in managing multiple projects to the extent that your group succeeds and, in turn, your group will succeed to the extent that they're perceived not merely as talented but also as reliable. It's not enough that certain members or parts of the group are reliable; reliability should be the goal of the group as a whole. As its manager, you hold the ultimate responsibility for the reliability of the group.

The only way for you to maintain that reliability is to be able, in principle, to track every single commitment the group makes. This requires systems that gather and maintain the information you need, while interfering with production work as little as possible.

We hope the ideas we've presented in this book will help you in this endeavor.

We also hope to set a good example by being open to criticism and suggestions for improvement, as well as to kudos and requests for further assistance. Please send your feedback to us at multiproj@ducks-in-a-row.com. We look forward to hearing from you.

Manager's Checklist for Chapter 12

❏ Workgroups are complicated systems that rely on complicated creatures—human beings. Understand that making changes to such a system will be frustrating at times.

❏ Establish your credibility as a change agent by starting with small but achievable changes. Look for a relatively easy change with relatively large payoffs. Go for the big changes only after you've proven that small changes can work.

❏ Compartmentalization is a way to stage changes. Focus on a sequence of changes for each compartment. Step through each identified change in each compartment until the entire workload is functioning under the new plan. This keeps the process of change moving at a reasonable pace, without the danger of attempting too much too fast and risking loss of credibility.

❏ Change takes time. It may be when you're at your busiest that the need for change is most evident, but that's a terrible time to add the stress of change to the load already in place. Wait until there's sufficient slack to accommodate the extra work of the change effort.

❏ Include your team in the process of planning your new systems, procedures, and/or routines. Take their concerns seriously. Not only is their buy-in critical to the success of the change process, but they understand the nature of the work and have a great deal of valuable insight to contribute.

❏ Be open to staff complaints as the new systems get under way. Even with your best efforts, you may not have thought of every implication or difficulty that could arise. Identify snags, recall the specific objectives you had in mind as you put these changes into effect, and address the problems with solutions that serve your objectives.

❏ You and your work group will succeed if you prove to be not just capable, but above all reliable. There's no universal recipe for reliability, but in this book you've found some useful strategies to consider.

Useful Books to Find Out More

M uch of the material in this book is original, but we draw our inspirations from many sources. Here are some of the books we found most useful. You may find them inspiring as well.

Getting Things Done: The Art of Stress-Free Productivity
David Allen
Viking Press, 2001
Allen argues for personal time management that is airtight. One of the best approaches to time management, and an excellent primer for the material in this book.

The Complete Idiot's Guide to Project Management
Sunny Baker and Kim Baker
Alpha Books, 1998
Like the other books in the "Complete Idiot" series, this book is really intended for the intelligent novice. It is a friendly and broad introduction to the issues of managing a large, complex project. Especially useful for the beginning manager is the material on task breakdowns and generating network diagrams.

Roundtable on Project Management
James Bullock, Gerald M. Weinberg and Marie Benesh, eds.
Dorset House, 2001
Thought-provoking and sometimes amusing discussions among experienced software project managers. Some of the thoughts are particular to software, and some are particular to very large projects, but there are nuggets here for any manager. It's always useful to watch people who think about process for a living think about process.

Home Office Handbook
Barbara Butler
Hungry Minds Press, 2001
While focused on the home office/small office marketplace, and unabashedly biased in favor of Hewlett-Packard products where possible, this book offers an excellent overview of the state of contemporary office technology. The ambitious manager would do well to read a book of this sort carefully every few years to keep up with the tricks of the trade.

Flow: The Psychology of Optimal Experience
Mihaly Csikszentmihalyi
Harper Collins, 1991
In this book, a professor of psychology draws on research and anecdote to argue that people are happiest when they are presented with an appropriate level of challenge, one that is neither too severe nor too modest. Keep this in mind while you are managing, and your team will be at its best.

Slack: Getting Past Burnout, Busywork, and the Myth of Total Efficiency
Tom DeMarco
Broadway Books, 2001
This provocatively titled book is getting Tom DeMarco some of the recognition that he deserves outside the narrow world of software management. DeMarco points out the flaws and fallacies inherent in expecting every minute of work time to be explicitly goal-oriented.

Peopleware: Productive Projects and Teams
Tom DeMarco and Timothy Lister
Dorset House, 1987
This book focuses on creating a creative workplace culture. It rue-
fully describes how high-value-added workplaces often make
penny-wise pound-foolish decisions, and insists on a workplace
that supports the creative worker. The section where they measure
the cost of interruptions on productivity and reliability should be
required reading for managers everywhere.

The Juggler's Guide to Managing Multiple Projects
Michael Dobson
Project Management Institute, 1999
The only prior publication we could find on the subject at hand,
this book focuses on formal project management principles and
how they can be extended to the multiple project environment.
This book is at its strongest in discussing formal methods for environments with a few large projects drawing on common resources,
but it addresses other situations as well.

Successful Time Management: A Self-Teaching Guide
Jack Ferner
John Wiley & Sons, 1995
An excellent guide to personal time management techniques, with
detailed exercises and example forms, this book also touches on
delegation and teamwork issues.

*The E-Myth Revisited: Why Most Small Businesses Don't Work
and What to Do About It*
Michael Gerber
Harper Collins, 1995
The "E-Myth" or entrepreneur's myth is the belief that a technical
core competency is sufficient to run a business. His solution provides an excellent example of the power of compartmentalization.

Time Tactics of Very Successful People
B. Eugene Griessman
McGraw-Hill, 1994
While almost any other resource can be bought, even the most
successful people have to cope with the fact that there are only 24

hours in a day. As a result, time is the most precious commodity for ambitious people. This book is full of suggestions for making every minute count. Not every idea is for everyone, but there is something for every situation in this compendium, and the overall idea is invaluable.

Project Management
Gary R. Heerkens
McGraw-Hill, New York, 2002
Another title in the Briefcase Books series, this is a down-to-earth how-to book for beginners in project management. It looks at the role of the project manager, project planning, dealing with risk and uncertainty, control, interfacing with stakeholders, and bringing the project to a successful conclusion.

Simplify Your Workday
Barbara Hemphill and Pamela Quinn Gibbard
Reader's Digest Press, Pleasantville, NY, 1998
Most books on work life are conceptual, but this one is highly visual. It offers numerous wonderful photographs and illustrations of well-designed work spaces. It offers inspiration as to how office work can be structured to be a pleasant and productive experience.

Smart Questions: The Essential Strategy for Successful Managers
Dorothy Leeds
Berkley Press, New York, 1987
Leeds offers an extensive introduction to the art of asking questions, whether of subordinates, supervisors, or peers, as a tool to advance an ambitious career. She helps the reader develop a sense of which questions are too dangerous, which questions are too likely to close off conversation, and the happy medium that extracts the maximum amount of information.

Fundamentals of Project Management
James P. Lewis
AMACOM, 1997
A quick tour of formal project management fundamentals, with a detailed explanation of the PERT process, including best/worst case analysis.

Why Change Doesn't Work: Why Initiatives Go Wrong and How to Try Again—and Succeed
Harvey Robbins and Michael Finley
Peterson's, 1996
An examination of the causes and consequences of resistance to change within an organization, as well as some of the unfortunate results of previous failures, this book offers practical advice for trying again and succeeding despite the odds.

Breaking Out of the Change Trap
Ron Rosenberg
Banbury Press, 1997
This practical guide to organizational change presents a step-by-step process for planning, promoting, and implementing change in a wide variety of settings.

The Leader's Handbook: A Guide to Inspiring Your People and Managing the Daily Workflow
Peter R. Scholtes
McGraw-Hill, 1998
An excellent contribution to the "quality" movement, this book is an in-depth study of how the manager gets things done effectively and reliably. It examines several of the ideas presented in this book in depth.

Operations Management
Jae K. Shim and Joel G. Siegel
Barron's Educational Series, 1999
A business school type overview of the concepts and strategies of operations management, this book contains an excellent introduction to the PERT process.

To Do, Doing, Done: A Creative Approach to Managing Projects and Effectively Finishing What Matters Most
G. Lynne Snead and Joyce Wycoff
Fireside Press, 1997
A nice book in the Franklin Covey school of time management, clear and not too wordy or preachy. A good example of the genre, it's systematic, but puts too much emphasis on prioritization and not enough on decision.

Rapid Problem Solving with Post-it® Notes
David Straker
Fisher Books, 1997
More than just a pitch for a well-known office product, this book serves as a wonderful and accessible introduction to systems thinking. There is no better introduction to the process of going from a vague set of ideas to a formal process.

The Information Paradox: Realizing the Business Benefits of Information Technology
John Thorp and DMR's Center for Stategic Leadership
McGraw-Hill, 1996
Why does information technology amount to a huge net gain in some companies and a huge net loss in others? Making the best use of information is a skill, and the new technological components make it more so. This book addresses the issue broadly at a corporate level.

Index

chatilasbakery.com